P.E.N.
New Poetry II

P.E.N.
New Poetry II

Edited by Elaine Feinstein

QUARTET BOOKS
London   New York

First published by Quartet Books Limited 1988
A member of the Namara Group
27/29 Goodge Street
London W1P 1FD

British Library Cataloguing in Publication Data

P.E.N. new poetry.
2
1. Poetry in English, 1945– –Anthologies
I. Feinstein, Elaine, 1930–II. PEN
821'.914'08

ISBN 0–7043-2659-0

Typeset by MC Typeset Ltd, Chatham, Kent
Reproduced, printed and bound in Great Britain by
Hazell Watson & Viney Limited
Member of BPCC plc
Aylesbury Bucks

Contents

Foreword

Old themes repeat as always: love, loss, the fear of death, children and old age. If there has been a change in emphasis, it lies in the use of personal experience almost exclusively. There are very few political poems, though there were a number of descriptions of a harsh life in England now. One of the pleasures of editing such an anthology has been the wide variety of other people's voices and lives it allowed me to enter. Few writers these days, it seems, stand solemnly in front of scenery which they hope will engender a poem.

Here is a rich trawl of poets ranging from established favourites such as Dannie Abse, Vernon Scannell, Ruth Fainlight and Anne Stevenson to poets whose names are unknown. Some were regulars who have contributed to earlier anthologies. Among the newest voices are those who have recently won prizes elsewhere. Those who submitted poems which have not been included were often of very high calibre, and almost every would-be contributor seemed aware of contemporary poetry which might once not have been the case; very few of them were archaic in diction, or embarrassing in rhythm. What was hardest was to sort out the almost-good-enough from those I finally chose. Probably all choices are unfair, eccentric and based on the mood of an editor. Some poems suffered from having another, clearly much better poem on the same theme already selected.

It is some evidence for the satisfactions of shaping experience into poetry that so many people should give such serious attention to doing so, often with wit and passion. The craftsmanship suggests more people are reading poetry these days than for a long time; perhaps more than at any time since the war. I have no social guess about why this is so, but I cannot believe it is only a question of marketing.

ELAINE FEINSTEIN

P.E.N.
New Poetry II

Dannie Abse

OF TWO LANGUAGES

For Hanoch Bartov

I
Citizen Dov walking on Mount Carmel
heard Agnon speaking Yiddish to a companion.
'How can you,' complained Dov, 'a five-star scholar,
a great *Hebrew* author, a Nobel-prize winner,
prophet amongst men, Solomon amongst Kings,
a genuine, first-class somebody (destined for
a State Funeral) how can *you* speak Yiddish?'

'Observe which way we're walking,' replied Agnon.
'Downhill. Downhill, I always speak Yiddish.
Uphill – break forth into singing, ye mountains –
uphill, I speak the language of Isaiah.'

II
Dov, you know Hebrew, you also know Yiddish.
Did you not speak to God in Hebrew
when you spoke to men in Yiddish?

All those used-up, ascetic centuries
of studying the evidence of 22 consonants;
the 23rd would not have destroyed the world.

Now in Hebrew, bellicose, you say, 'Go away.'
Once, softly in Yiddish, you begged, 'Leave me alone.'

Tell me, what's the word for 'mercy' in Hebrew?
In Yiddish, 'mercy' must have many synonyms.

3

Say now in Yiddish: 'Exile. Pogrom. Wandering.
   Holocaust.'
Say now in Hebrew: 'Blessed Art Thou O Lord.'

A CONSPICUOUS COUPLE

Bubbles, brass, gaudy things, they loved well,
all that glitters and is starred,
the seven fairground colours swanking
on the bevelled edge of glass –
she, dramatic as a sunset,
he, chromatic like a rainbow
or an oilpool in the yard.

Love, agog, italic, rang their bell:
her computer flashing like a million,
he, randy, sighing like a villain;
she spread, he swooped, a kingfisher,
a kind of flying oilpool –
how they fluttered, how they fired,
till they guttered on her bed.

Naughty Aphrodite (minus nightie)
surely blessed them when they married,
outstaining the stained church window;
not the spermless priest who muttered,
'With this paintbox I thee wed,
a sunset to a rainbow
or an aurora borealis.'

The best man's innuendoes –
he was importune and loaded;
the aunts goofy and embarrassed
for no kiss could be more sexy
to erect in church a boudoir.
And big the triumph of the organ
when, promptly, the choirboys exploded.

SMILING THROUGH

'All great art is praise.' John Ruskin

I
Then there's the parable of three wise men
(always three, as in a joke), who walk
in their fresh linen through the sweet morning
till they hear fat busy flies, see a dog,
stiff legs in the air disintegrating.
'What a terrible sight!' cries the first beard.
'What a terrible smell!' complains the second.
'What lovely white teeth,' the third, rapturously.

II
The scandalous paradox of cripples
and slums in a world of colours.

Praise the white tooth.

The expensive bombs blessed with holy cries
falling on the screams of mothers.

Praise the white tooth.

III
Meanwhile, sky in narrow streets;
yet turning the hands of a clock,
as one might do at bedtime
(though it is only afternoon)
something may fall away or arrive:
another place, a beautiful
virus-free clearing where, of course,
everybody is so happy
not least the three up-market shepherds
everything grassy and bird-song,
flower-pretty and river sound,
the sky blue blue blue everywhere
over this landscape waiting for

a Poussin. But look – in the dark
green shadow of that light green tree
a human skull, teeth in its jaw
uttering, 'I, too, am in Arcady.'

IV
The famine babies with ponderous eyes
in a careless world of plenty.

Praise the white tooth.

The future with chernobyl disease
in one year or in twenty?

Praise the white tooth.
Praise the white tooth.

Anna Adams

THE RUCKSACK

I bend to no more prams, I walk upright
as hands-in-pockets man; I will not haul
great sacks of washing to the launderette,
or bags of shopping home, nor cans of oil;
others may still lean sideways from the weight
of baskets full of bottles, bread and fruit,
or backwards from the bulging womb in front,
drag children by the hand, and push and pull
wheelchairs and shopping-trolleys, but I won't.
I'm through with lugging burdens up the street;
even this token handbag I resent.

And yet I bear a rucksack on my back,
unseen, but full of leaden bric-a-brac
collected in the past; it makes me stoop
although I stand erect, it bends my neck;
I bow down to the fact I can't unstrap
this incubus, put up with it, forget
just what it is that presses on my nape
much like a hump. If once I could escape
I'd levitate, but the magnetic ground
tugs downward. Sorrows of my mother's kind
sit hard on me and make my shoulders round.

In bed each night, before my dreams take over,
I grope into the rucksack, separate
the closepacked objects, feel them like a lover,
but can't discover if they're bones or baubles.
Hot shrapnel, striking sparks from pavingstones
during loud air-raids, had such jagged shapes;
some pierce my hands like serpents' teeth, but sharper;

some feel as smooth as seaworn granite pebbles,
but harder, heavier; the heaviest
is made of inextricably compressed
lost burdens that I carried in time past.

INVASION AND CONQUEST OF THE COTTAGE

After three hundred years
of shepherds, gamekeepers and quarrymen:
of conscientious housewives – washing, baking,
scrubbing and polishing and patchwork-making,
and giving birth upstairs
to servants, dry-stone wallers, railwaymen –
this house can't know what's hit it: Germans, Cockneys,
gallery directors, poets, Hockneys,
publishers and critics and au-pairs.

John Adlard

KRYSTYNA SAID:

That was a summer of fat blue flies. They teased
Dry mouths and moist wounds of the living and dead.
October came, Warsaw surrendered,
The secret army emerged dispirited;
But my father hid in a cellar and over his head,
In a hole blasted when the building fell,
A pram hung with a perfect blonde doll
Beside it, upside down. For a week he hid
And then he remembered he had friends in Łódź.
Should he go to Łódź? He had nowhere else to go.

Across Poland he went in the autumn weather,
Through dull forests and frightened villages,
Avoiding the high-roads of course. And one morning
He stood in the centre of Łódź and rubbed his eyes
And slapped himself to be sure it wasn't a dream;
For the trams were gliding along, the mills were working
And in the cafés fat, wealthy women were choosing
Cakes and cream or coffee and fresh rolls,
With their beautiful, silly daughters on display,
As he stood there, a stinking bag of bones.

It was no dream. The explanation was simple –
Stalin knew how to preserve a productive town.
Then my father learned a lesson of history,
That the heroes have no say. If you stumble home
Alone, where a legion strutted out that morning,
If you travel to Hell and bring back only a poem,
And you strive to explain glory and degradation
To ears content with a music that's easy and loud,
To eyes blind to the logic of sacrifice,
Your orations will serve to amuse a strolling crowd.

Brian Aldiss

THE TWENTIETH CAMP: For Elaine Feinstein

All the centuries were on display across the plain,
Each closely guarded, wired, and separated from the next.
And yet, despite the dogs and floodlights, people made their
    way
Beyond the barricades, going in fear and fugitive,
Each subject to inherited blind promptings to survive.

Inside these gulags stretching to infinity we saw –
And did not cease to marvel as we looked – how every one
Contained a circumscribed diversity of love and hate.
The strikers and the struck, the givers and the ones who
    took,
Praying or cursing, some forsaken, others who forsook.

A fearful beauty in the camps prevailed. Some folk
    maintained
A gentle air throughout all punishment. Among the eyes
That challenged us, dark in their violence, a few there were
Which shone compassion: men and women who, behind
    their bars
Immured, sustained a spirit almost free. Yet all bore scars.

When to the largest of these fearsome camps we came, we
    cried,
'How is it that this Twentieth brims with so much despair,
Much more oppression, famine, war, and mouths stopped in
    their prime?'
The answer came: 'Your knowledge without wisdom cannot
    save,
And Man, enslaving all of nature, is himself a slave.'

Connie Bensley

WANTS

Like yours, my wants are simple:
security with the window ajar,

the battle without the spilt guts;
the family to throw off

and rediscover; a magical bedpost
and Life Everlasting, with my own teeth.

Anne Blonstein

THE VIRGIN SALLY

I

She was never able to draw a really straight line.
That, she thought, was madness, as she skirted
The word-polluted pond rather than sink

To its stagnant centre. She would not conform
Or perform as an aristocrat's daughter
Should. She could not be steered into the main stream

But was as essential to the plot as the clotting agent
Rushing to the torn defences of the tender wound:
It is foolish to apply leeches to the spirit.

II

Innocents and old maids, children and mad women
Stare at people as at a pantomime. For this they are
    reproached.
They must be made to understand that there are no lesbians

Amongst the gay young buggers, you must fall in love
With man. A dizzy heretic, she trembled on the banks of the
    Thames
While it oozed lugubrious through the debris of war.

III

Long, long ago she had been dropped. Her high shoulder,
A sign that they murder unwanted second daughters,
Was bruised, but not perfectly broken.

IV

Cracked mirrors return crazy reflections.
Silver trapped behind glass always repeating,
Always, always the daughter imitates her mother's manner

So exactly. While others only see
What they want to: themselves reflected
In her transparent eyes and spasmodic gestures,

In the clown's mime, the ventriloquist's silent speech.
Her echoes echo foolishness. Absently she quotes
Someone else's lyrics, tunelessly she hums someone else's
    song.

V

The fifth sign of madness is writing for yourself.
Let your obsessions fill the stage with actresses,
But beware accepting a ready-made script.

VI

For once upon a time there was an anorexic princess
Who dared to defy her father. He buried her
Alive. She twitched like an unexploded bomb

Wrapped in the bleeding mud of Flanders.
Poisoned by the first party she played truant from the last,
Fleeing dreams of rape while her ashes rained on London.

Alison Brackenbury

ON MIDSUMMER DAY

I have heard their voices, from a country
shaken by tractors, burdened by empty rooms:
where small apples fell untasted in the gardens.

They did not come at Hallowe'en, in the blind rain.
In the broad heat of June they walked from the wood
where dog's mercury huddled in poisonous crowds.
As at rest from work, they sat on the field's margin
with hay heaped green, its flowers still to finger,
gilt of buttercups, purple dust of heartsease:
small pansies starred more open than their faces.

Beneath thick skirts and hems I saw their boots
pale with dust of summer, turning tender feet
of men and women rough and burning.
I knew that they had tramped round farms for work –
now the towns flood people –
that the apple tree, self-sown,
dropped misshapen bobbins, soft and tasteless.
House walls still run with damp. What can be new?

'As I came to the wood, wheat broke,' I said,
'into white ripples from a sound. They hung
red signs upon the gate which cried out "Danger!"
I heard a shotgun blast among the trees.'

'There was always shooting in the woods,' they said.
'If we had guns we would have shot there too.'

So the gap fell between us, the old shadow,
Raw and new. A gun boomed, far away.

14

Out of the hot June evening, the air trembled.
Rain would come. White willows at the wood's edge
Flickered silence.

'Just before you came,
out of wild grass, red docks, flowered nettles –'
I spoke of nothing, but to keep them there –
'a dragonfly flashed by, its wings pure black.
Its body shook light-blue. Then snowy moths,
all foreign creatures from the shortest summer.'

'Yes.' Eyes creased, they nodded.

'Do you mean
that you have seen it? But you are my people
from the flat land's blank corn –'

'There were still woods.'

'But it was never there! Just now, I came
alone up this broad slope through whitening stalks
where quick wings came; then left me. You were dead.'

The guns fell quiet. Wings shivered, thin black heat.
'Look. Here is the dragonfly,' they said.

The spider walks across the air
He curls a long foot round his thread
His legs, brown-striped in sunlit grass
Jerk, as wakened from the dead.

So I; at last released from work
Can sit beside the unwashed glass,
See the slow spider stalk through space
Until a green half-hour has passed.

Then, as he twists and firms the thread
There swerves in me this sudden joy
Although his lightness turns a trap
Though all he makes there, will destroy.

Alan Brownjohn

AN ORDINARY PLAYER

Today's choice for surgery glides past
With a wave and a request: 'Brass handles, please!'
The surgeon's lips will smile inside his mask,
The anaesthetist's hat is a perky white
Like a fast food chef's.
                                        Late in the afternoon
He glides back, waking, as the January
Darkness renders us our long clean room
In coloured windows: blue sisters read
Our records, and a witness nurse stares down
At the red pills shaken in the dice-cup.

With the supper done, we shuffle up our chairs
To allow a space: including in the deal
One other player, to be entertained
Because he is too close for discomfort,
And far too ordinary to fend off
With superstition.
                                        Still he has not won
When the ceiling lights dim out and the pictures fade,
And we return to bed, passing the table
Where the coloured pieces of the Monster
Puzzle lie half-unsolved in the half-dark.

When the cat fled past like a running cushion,
And vanished into the images on the screen,
I dropped my cup. The splash of coffee made
A wider stain on the flagstones than seemed
Quite possible, a large, seared cat-shape
We could not erase for some time. And the cup smashed.
So I said: Take the bits out into the garden
And deposit them with the rest. Our family is
Accustomed to responding with fright or shock
If a fire recalls its burning, and the flames
Die back to kindling wood and unlit coals;
And accustomed to breaking a plate, or bowl, or dish
If one walks upstairs with it during a heat wave noon
And opens a bedroom window onto moonlit snow . . .
We are thoroughly used to whatever happens here;
Which is why our garden is a rubbish trove
Of crockery pieces back to toga times
And beyond them, to broken arrows and fumbled flints.
So I said: Drop the fragments out in the garden,
And I will stroll along the long gallery,
Calling my ancestors severally out of their frames
To assemble on the terrace. In tall-heeled boots,
And buckled shoes, and sandals, and callused feet,
They shall tread the patterned pieces into the ground.

Elizabeth Burns

GOING BACK TO CHAPELTON

July, barefoot, she is running outside
for breathfuls of the clean breezy air that ruffles
the sycamore, brushes the fur of the barley
while the valley full of pastel fields
is lit by the passing of pale sun
that drifts through clouds to Dunsinane.

Here at the border between garden and farm
they plant out little cabbages
opal leaves flopping onto black soil
and unearth yellowed pebbles of potatoes
and carrots, wrinkled and minute as babies' fingers:
witchlike, she slices them in with the peas

startled emerald and sweet from their pods;
then there are bowlfuls of scarlet strawberries
unwashed, earthy, rough against the tongue
until teeth bite the slice of pink.
They eat them by the crackle of applewood fire
summer and winter jarred together

and she is dreaming back to how it was before
snow feet-deep around the cottage
iced air frosting your throat as you breathe
and how that evening they talked and drank
in the close circle of the fire, fed flames
that glanced on flagons of elderflower wine

and so covered by the snow of love were they,
thinking its blanket of beauty and oblivion
would never melt as they held close

19

to warm flesh and woke entwined
to sun skimming through iced glass,
that they never dreamt of passion's thaw.

Mellowed melted summer is gentle:
marigolds at the door, a nestling of herbs
rosemary, erica, borage, sage
lupins seeded and the raspberries become
soft rows of ripe fruit
where then they were bare canes stalking the snow.

But she wishes not for this slack fecund laziness
of summer months where there is no needlepoint sharpness
to the light, but remembers and weeps for
the weight and delight of snow
its sheer icing and stabs at the heart
of stalactite.

Richard Burns

Three extracts from THE MANAGER

I have spent much of my time looking for a small piece of joy I seem to have lost somewhere. Maybe in early childhood.

Like the jigsaw piece I dropped there. And it wedged between floorboards. And trying to prise it out I pushed it further in.

And heard it drop between rafters. And splintered my right forefinger. And with a stolen needle extracted the wood-sliver

And did not flinch or call but grinned at my squeezed blood drop. And for that adult grimace

Under gritted milkteeth, the loss of that wedge of innocence, my last cardboard clue to complete

And seal perfection – seemed small price, seemed nothing. Till now my strengths numb me. My silences conspire against me.

My secrets bar me out. My grin tortures my soul. I am least at home in my home. Memories erode my vision. And I am sick with longing

To stride back in that house. Obtain present owner's permission. Pull up his carpet and underfelt. Wrench his floorboards up

And find that missing fragment of dusty cobwebbed cardboard. With its faded bit of picture

Of sail and sea on its good side. And wear it on a chain in a locket. And treasure its golden presence.

But I have dredged the dream and lost the address of that child. Hey What's Your Name. Can you help. I can't remember. As usual.

★ ★ ★

I have searched all over this house. Through lobby lounge and loft. Between leaves of books. In every cupboard and closet. Even behind mirrors. I have dredged the dream and the day. For you who were

Wholly perpetual are traceless as melted snow. Gone companions of honour from fastnesses of my kinghood and farthest regions of radiance, you who were angels once with no dust specks on your wings,

Where are you. Come back. You, last lost jigsaw piece dropped under infancy's floorboards. Deeper than a dandelion rooted between two pavement slabs. And I guilty of cutting off your head.

And you, crayoned paper clown. Giant taller than cedar or redwood to me. My dragon and monster slayer. And best dream defender. Your spiky blazoned smile and bright hair crumpled ash.

And you, brave lead warrior who sank into our garden pond. To report back to surface tied to a length of string. Whose cable snapped in that nether world. Where still you lie drowning.

And you, silver cufflinks inherited from my father. Gone awol when I last looked in your red leather box. And a gong hammer hit my heart and went on resounding through. For I'd clambered

Onto his lap and toyed with you at his sleeve ends. And said, Dad. When you die. What will happen to these. And he'd laughed and said, Son. Whatever I have. I promise. One day will be yours.

Hey you, I call. Gone presences: now figments dulled in

camouflage or, varnished, shells and shards, well meshed
into the backgrounds of things: your shapeless glimmers and
reckonings, your screens

And unbeckoning blindspots, silent desert valleys and
sheen-scratched patches of mist: unhuntable chameleons,
what language do you speak these days, who lived through
so many forms: each hallmarked

Perfection. Aren't you there, I call. Angels. Won't you
please come in now. But my line to the dead has been
disconnected. No sound comes back from the pillow or
interceding dark.

* * *

TELEX

212973 BUNGUM G
KEY+0223249432+
249432 BONKAM G
212973 BUNGUM G

212973   29/2   SUX

ATTN PROSPECT INTERNATIONAL MANAGING
DIRECTOR & BOARD OF DIRECTORS

WITH REFERENCE AFOREMENTIONED ITEM
'JOY' BELIEVED BY ME PERSONALLY MISLAID
SOMEWHERE IN EARLY CHILDHOOD REGRET
CANNOT STATE ACCURATELY TIME DATE PLACE
OF LOSS OR MODE OR EXACT CIRCUMSTANCES
THEREOF

WHETHER BY DISAPPEARANCE METAMORPH-
OSIS THEFT BURGLARY OR OTHER FORM OF
MISAPPROPRIATION BY NOXIOUS AGENCY OR
PERSON OR PERSONS UNKNOWN WITH OR WITH-
OUT PREJUDICE OR OTHER UNSPECIFIED CAUSE
WHATSOEVER

SINCE MOTIVE FOR SUCH SEEMS INEXPLICABLE
ACCORDING TO BOTH COMMON SENSE AND ALL
CITED INTERPRETATIONS OF RELEVANT RE-

SEARCH INTO CASES DOCUMENTED BOTH
PATHOLOGICAL AND NONPATHOLOGICAL
BEARING IN MIND

NONTRANSFERABILITY OF ASSET IN QUESTION
WITHOUT CONSCIOUS AWARENESS SUBLIMINAL
SUSPICION OR AT LEAST PERIPHERAL REGISTRA-
TION OF EXCHANCE HANGOVER OR SOBSTITU-
TION PROGRESS ON PART OF CURRENT INCUM-
BENT

NOR CAN I ANYWHERE FIND NOR HAVE IN MY
POSSESSION RELEVANT RECEIPTS INVOICES
CHECKSTUBS PLASTIKARD STATEMENTS
VOUCHERS DEEDS WARRANTIES OR OTHER
PROOFS OF PURCHASE OR DOCUMENTATION OF
LEASE OR OWNERSHIP

AND SINCE NONE OF MY ONGOING POLICIES
SPECIFIES COVERAGE FOR SUCH RISK FACTOR
OR EVENTUALITY UNDER ANY CLAUSE OR SUB-
SECTION NOR INDEED COULD BE INTERPRETED
AS LIKELY TO DO SO BY ANY COMPETENT
ASSESSOR

I HAVE FILLED IN NO CLAIM FORMS FILED NO
POLICE REPORTS MADE NO COMPLAINTS
SIGNED NO PETITIONS BUT CARRIED ON AS
USUAL ATTEMPTING WITHOUT MISDEMEANOUR
OR DISTURBANCE TO KEEP MY AFFAIRS IN
ORDER

WHEREFORE BEING OF SOUND CHEER FIT DIS-
POSITION AND ACCORDING TO CURRENT MODES
IN MY RIGHTFUL MIND AM PREPARED TO
ACCEPT SUSTAIN AND UNDERTAKE TO FULFIL
TOTAL RESPONSIBILITY AND LIABILITY FOR
SAID LOSS

PROVIDED AND ON SOLE CONDITION YOU
GUARANTEE FULL ACKNOWLEDGEMENT THAT I
HAVE MADE EVERY POSSIBLE ATTEMPT EFFORT
AND INVESTIGATION IN MY POWER TO EFFECT

FULL RECOVERY OF AFORESAID ITEM NOT-
WITHSTANDING

RECURRENT PARTIAL AMNESIA ABSENCE
HOPELESSNESS PAIN RANCOR RAGE PARANOIA
DEPRESSION DESPAIR DESPONDENCY GRIEF
GUILT REGRET FEAR OF DEATH OF DYING
LONELINESS NUMBNESS AND ALL THEIR COM-
MON CONCOMITANTS AND PHYSICAL

SYMPTOMS AND SYNDROMES IN THEIR WHOLE
RANGE OF MANIFESTATIONS. SHOULD THIS IN-
FORMATION INVOLVE CONTRACT CANCELLA-
TIONS TENDER WITHDRAWALS OR SUSPENSION
OF OR HINDRANCE TO ANY ASPECTS SOEVER OF
OUR HITHERTO

CORDIAL AND MUTUALLY BENEFICIAL COL-
LABORATIONS PLEASE ADVISE FORTHWITH. I
HOPE HOWEVER ADEQUATE ALTERNATIVE OR
FAILING THAT AT LEAST SURROGATE ARRANGE-
MENTS CAN BE MADE FOR SATISFACTION OF
ALL CONCERNED PARTIES BRUNO.

JORDAN CHARLES BRUNO MAPLAN FLOATING
GHOST MANAGER MDDX PROSPECT NATIONAL
PLEASE CORRECT TLX ERRORS LINE 22 EXCH-
ANCE – EXCHANGE AND LINE 22 HANGOVER –
HANDOVER SOBSTITUTION – SUBSTITUTION
PROGRESS – PROCESS.

212973 BUNGUM G

Gillian Clarke

TROPHY

'Thorpe Satchville Beagles, 3 hours, Clawson, January 26th
   1928'

In the ice-trap of January
trees splinter a low sun
and the pond's brilliance
is glazed to pearl like the eye
of the old blind dog.

Hares start from furrows
to fire the land, their ears
small standing shadows, each bone
an instrument for listening,
each foot on the pulse of the earth.

Musk in the brain, the hounds
are a parliament of braying.
Of all creatures the hare
has the largest heart,
his blood-volume the greatest.

This one outran the pack
for a hare's nine lives,
and does again through an afternoon
when trees sing in ice, and air
is opal for three winter hours.

I heard of a hare who outran hounds
for a day and died of heartburst, found
at his death-moment, his arteries
full of air-bubbles instead of blood.

Or hares on aerodrome runways
racing the jets taking off.

When they cast the torn body away
and saved the golden head
for the taxidermist's shield,
in turn they emptied the horn
in the Star, Long Clawson.

At Thorpe Satchville the kennelman
set bowls before his pets,
and rubbed their coats
to their usual shining.

TIMES LIKE THESE

Too heavy-hearted to go walking
in beech-woods. At night the children's sleep
is racked by dreams. They wake crying of war.
Pushing a pram in 1961,
I remember how love weighed, anger shored
against helplessness, how we wrote letters
to the papers, raged at Strontium 90,
the bitter rain that stained our mother-milk.

Yet my daughter's beautiful,
and my daughter's daughter, even then printed
in the womb of the waking embryo,
now resolves into her elements.
Shadow on shining, here she comes dancing
through the bright window of ultra-sound,
fiercer than death and kicking to be born.

In times like these we should praise trees and babies
and take the children walking in beech-woods.

Elsa Corbluth

QUAKER MEETING HOUSE, MOSEDALE, CUMBRIA

God keeps a teashop underneath Blencathra.
His wife, goddess, has on a forties dress.
(Nearby, the rabbit woman of Mungrisedale
runs a Post Office in her rabbit house.)
Cool as a hermit's cave, stone barn of meeting,
sanctuary from the sun-bled mountain sides.
Oak forms three hundred years of silent sitting
have smoothed, rest the fell-weary. Little guides
to Peace lie on thick shelves; the dove motif
is pinned on badges, roosts on posters, hands,
those wings, in supplication. God's goodwife
offers the cakes. God, with his white beard, tends
the bubbling urn, like Moses tapping rock.
Out of a steaming cup the Spirit spoke:

god of the thirsty, dove of little Mosedale,
hovering in window light over the pale
dried grasses in stone jars on the deep sill,
oh ancient silent god of this small place,
arms oaken roof boughs, scalp of birdsong, please,
out of your stone and wood and shadows, days
and lives of patient waiting,
find us
peace.

John Cotton

Its name in gilt on shiny red rexine,
It stood out amongst the 'Cyclopaedia's green
And the glossy brown of the collected Dickens
(Free with a subscription to *John Bull*).
This do-it-yourself of the healing arts,
This alphabet of ailments, aches,
And, most importantly, of parts,
Was my deep and furtive reading
From which I learnt the nomenclature of sex,
When I could snatch a time with it alone:
Nipple, vulva, uterus.
Until one day I met big breasted Joan
And soon discarded all the fuss
Of names, to share a wonder very close to love.

Tony Curtis

THE SHUTTERS

I take a rotten photograph
I always have.

Mother, what the album shows again and again
is the three of us – two women separated
by a generation, a marriage bed
and a single, spoilt son.

We three pose at the backdoor –
you hold the pedal car I steer
but Gran perches my bear on the bonnet
and I'm looking at her.

Down our garden path at Pentrefelin
I threaten the flower border
toddling towards the camera
buffered at chest and bottom by her strong hands.

On the green at Llanstephan
I sit smiling, on the bench next to Gran
and, Mother, you are looking knives
into the side of her head.

Was that a minute before or after
the one that has me in the crook
of her broad arm, tickled while Dad jokes
to hold his pipe to her smoking ear?

In all those snaps
Gran took *a good photograph*
face set to the lens. A look
that unnerved my father's grip –

each print has strokes of wild light
that flamed through the clumsy shutter.
What shapes us is clear, developed, fixed tight.
The two of us are still there, Mother.

THE LOFT

I've made up me mind.
I'm packing the birds in,
the loft can go.
There's too much to do,
in the house, like
and outside. The lawn takes two
hours cutting, and the veg garden
. . . what do I want with all that veg?
There's company down the club, I know,
but I can't hear with that organ
going down there. The smoke
gets so bad you can't breathe.

No, I'll pack it in
back end of this year,
though I'm cock of the club this season –
Old Bird Average, Cross-Channel, Best Young Bird,
Gloucester Annual. I said
to them, give me one cup, like, one
big cup. Last season we had a box full
of them replicas – the case in there
won't take no more.
Where would I put them all?

Your mother used to clean them.
They used to shine.

Did she ever tell you how we met?
Knocked each other over in an air-raid.
I chased her up from seeing her uniform
and next day I took a lorry
and drove across to the hospital and parked

right outside and was meself chased
off by this matron – a real dragon she were,
I won't have the likes of soldiers
pestering my girls, she said.
Forty years ago and more.
Brought together we was, by the war.

I sold a good 'un this week.
Eight years a winner,
from a class sire and grandame,
his sons and daughters all winners.
I sold him back to the bloke that bred him.
Could have fetched a bit in the auction
– a hundred pounds or more.
Sold it back for thirty quid.
For stock.

Yes, it's been one of me best years.
I had one back the other week been
missing for two months. This lad sent
thirty-two birds to the same race
and never seen a feather, not a feather.
One of the top fanciers in the Fed.
A big crash it was, over the Channel from France.

That bird of mine come back like a good 'un.
From the East Coast, I shouldn't wonder.
Walked it. Picking grain
from the fields and making
his way all the time. They can
do that with it being harvest time,
barley crops mostly. They drop
and eat what's left. Course, then
he has to line himself up again.

No, I've had enough. There's too much to do.
Monday, I cleaned the cooker. Took me a good hour.
Under the rims, the grill-pan, all over.
Tuesday, I did the beds ready for you.
It's too much looking after the loft.

Your mother used to make me a cup
when I was watching out for them

and she'd help me –
d'you remember? –
bring 'em down and clock 'em in.
It's the time on the clock that counts.
Could be split seconds between winning
and nothing.

A year it'll be, next month.
In November.

GAMES WITH MY DAUGHTER

The first clear afternoon of Spring bursts
April's buds and bulbs in the park.
This year when I catch and take her weight
she powers the swing and arcs
from finger-stretch behind my head
to soaring feet-in-the-clouds.
Mothers to our left and right
shrink in their corridors of safe flight.

Our game's revealed the filling out,
the firmer, young woman's stare,
the promise Winter concealed beneath its coat.
Forward and up she splits the sky. Each
swing down and back she goes by to where
my tip-toed fingers' grasp can't reach.

Adrian Dannatt

A FISH BRIDE

Our days all flesh
until ocean-darkness drowns the bedside light
or salt mimics splintered diamond to the tongue.
Her body opens in drifts of hair
we play amorously at sub-aqueous lassitude
so deep below the sheet's low
canopy of white,
as if we'd drowned in sea of milk,
lactation not lust had stained us.

Sunlight trawls stairs to conquer
a sleep so black it calls on caverns,
blinds like empty postage stamps
rubbed thin with razor blade to hint at light
in this kingdom of fresh antiquity
with no victory but the clock,
no music but the breath,
only language, the pubic hair's neat scrawl.

Conch, eel and anchovy
scrub their set anatomy of smells
emergent from the sandy bed
of breakfast crumbs,
and dance an odorous polka
with ever louder sounding-depths
call in the nets!

Her tresses wander in the cotton valleys
left behind by sunken scale
skin dries and crumbles like crinkle chips,
aged in mortal minutes and cut by hessian weals
traced by the viciousness of slumberdown.

What a drenching and a pleasure!
It started as a port in any storm
then battened down its ocean hatches
became a coastal village fat with treasure.

Vincent De Souza

GOOD OLD CHURCHES

Churches pass for roundabouts now.
There's one bang in the centre of town,
In Richmond, Yorkshire.
A busy road circles around it,
And on the island itself
There are parked cars right up to the walls.
It saves people having to walk too far.
They can stroll to the shops
And come back to put their things in the boot.
And when they do, they can look up
And check the time on the church clock.
Some of them wonder if it's an antiques fair
Or a jumble sale inside.
There's a church in Norwich that's a scout hut,
Another that's a museum,
And one in Wymondham, Norfolk, is a library.
After all, Christ is getting on a bit,
And unused buildings are a crying shame.
You can't live in the past.
You can't resurrect a thing forever.

(Either that, or the cars and people are flies around the
wrong corpse. The church is like the lie of the land.)

Tim Dowley

EARLY LOSS

They shut my mother in her bedroom
drew the curtains
stole in and out.

A nurse took me to a wintry park
stopped my pushchair by the swans
fed sugar through the wire

to steaming deer.
She said she'd like to keep me
if they'd let her.

After the doctor's visit
Grandma presented a black Bible
promising it would last me years.

Later they allowed me in
'See your new sister!'
Mother, still there, sighed.

Stephen Duncan

IMPRINT

He noticed the snow,
hardened by night frost,
had all these:
fox, badger, heron,
triangle, lozenge, diamond,
in crisp intaglio
hard as printer's steel
– a babble of night signs.

Inside the cow barn,
dark and sour,
steam rose from crusted bellies,
black polished eyes
gleamed inside split husks
at the small boy.
She stamped backward
into her dung,
her calf pulling
on long swollen teats,
lips running white
slobbering milk.
Adjusting her thighs
a torrent of hot urine
poured into the concrete canal.
Black skin peeled open
for the wet pink folds,
an emerging flower,
and then contracted
with the fading stream.
He trembled.

Now, a man,
he stands in her warm room
for the first time,
watching as she turns
her sleepy body
and parts her legs.

FINAL SURRENDER

Post-war streets were like a jaw
gap toothed from a brawling fight.
Two rooms in a Munich tenement,
he pointed to the budgie in a cage
and his boozy 'mamma' with crooked teeth
and a German I couldn't follow.

Waved away we ran to the movies,
war films, the surrender to the Allies.
Explosions rocked the air,
concertined a pall of dust
as a fire ball descended the dug out steps,
with a phosphorescence brighter than sunlight,

our jackets burst into flames as we watched.
Full of the foyer's gum and cucken
cycling through the Mercedes and G.I. chevies,
he led me to the gang's 'headquarters',
an abandoned demolition site;
a bunker the last bastion of the Reich.

At each turn of the rubble packed track
following the edges of ruined cellars,
plump Bavarian boys stood to attention
and saluted as I passed. Armies quiet,
the meeting was held by candlelight,
old enemies too exhausted now to kill.

I received their surrender with dignity,
we shook hands as boys should

relieved to be still alive.
Curious of my power we experimented a wrestle,
smearing teeshirts in crumbling red brick,
arms locked in combat, brow to eye.

BLACK PLUMS

That year, a sweltering June,
groaning up the stairs from the market,
you brought back a heavy load
of fruit and veg, a bargain bag
of ripe plums, the press of damp bulges
tearing through the brown paper.

An old friend, he expired
at the peak of the summer's heat.
I saw his body packaged in a shroud
on the cool slab,
a face without response of any kind,
the flesh collapsed, sagging within.

Our summer holiday with nothing
but a towel around the waist
we ate fruit and drank the juice.
I held you, stroked your burnt skin,
searching for something new,
curves inside your swimsuit.

Those plums sat in their bowl
up in our high attic flat
while we stayed away.
An over-ripened dying body,
the brown flesh splitting skins
leaked a dark funereal juice.

Anthony Edkins

A CONVERSATION ABOUT NOSTALGIA

She accused him of nostalgia.

No, he assured her, not exactly that,
there's no longing to go back – to be back
there in the past – no, it's more a matter
of material, seams to be mined, ore
to be purified, marketed . . .
Nostalgia's something else:
an unappeasable yearning
that's treason to today;
it's as childish as dreams of talking to
Caesar in an anachronistic train;
nostalgia's reactionary,
a pettiness that always comes apart
below the surface of a superficial heart.

She seemed surprised, she did not look convinced,
she thought such vehemence suggested guilt –
uneasiness at least – about the role
the past played in his present: consider
how it crops up every time we talk –
yours, I mean, of my past you know nothing.

It made him pause; he wanted to argue
that secrecy was the opposite, not
of nostalgia but of the garrulous
assumption that history (meaning his)
was always interesting per se.

It could be, she admitted, sometimes *is*.

The same, he thought, could well be said
of your incessant chatter about the present
which negates both past and future
as surely as nostalgia denies now.

He *thinks* they laughed and kissed, touched hands,
went their separate ways.
She *knows* they pursed their lips, shook hands,
went their separate ways.
Neither's wrong, nor is either right:
the day is long but longer is the night.

Ruth Fainlight

FLIES

November sun as warm as a Levantine
winter made me push my window up
this morning, brought back donkey-drivers' calls,
the look and smell of bakers' stalls and offal
butchers. (Flies were everywhere.)

But the shudder of glass (fear a splintering shard
might pierce me) from the frame I carelessly jammed askew,
as heavy lorries brake and lower gear
to take the corner for a shortcut to the A40,
changed those images to Home County:
a pan of clarifying sugar syrup
on the Aga wrinkling as it starts to boil
(the crab-apple jelly-bag dripping draws flies
to the kitchen) or the irritable twitch
of a horse's flank to shift the biting flies.

The noise I heard could have been
the drone of a distant combine-harvester,
a helicopter spraying, or closer still
here in town, a treadle-machine next door
(that new family must be tailors) with their
muffled hullabaloo through the party wall (they're
killing each other: the flies are driving them crazy).

So I went to put the window down, to stop
the thrumming and its associations, and found
summer's last fly, trapped by the double-glazing.

THE FISH

Trying to think it through
force my mind to hold one specific
thought, makes my brain convulse and twist in my
skull like a fish in a net, with a fish's vigour.

I see the fixed glare of its eye – blood,
jet, and mica – feel the rasping touch
of fin and scale against my hand, the tail's
last spiny flick and panic-thrust
as it wrenches free; and I am left wondering
what it was I tried to think about, depleted

yet glad that now I can follow it through
all the way to the sea.

AUGUST

August is like a woman who's already thinking
that she'll soon be forty. There's something old-fashioned
about her, emanating a womanly odour
of sachets. You can tell that she's been badly treated
by men. Her daughter has left home. She's probably
divorced. She's the manageress of a dress shop.

One might talk of her carriage: she seems to be wearing
a corset. She's quite large and very white skinned.
Her hair is set, her face is powdered matt, and her
thin and rather mournful little mouth with lips
firmly closed on each other except when she bites
them, is carefully painted and always looks wet.

August is the month when everything stops growing.
She feels she stopped growing a long time ago – though

she wouldn't put it like that. She doesn't believe in
too much introspection. Dignified and solitary,
she walks through the park after work, under
the heavy, dusty, dying green of August trees.

FACTS AND FICTIONS

How many killings on the television?
How much spilled blood? How many bodies?
How exactly did that movie finish?
Next morning I've forgotten.

But certain images do not fade.
Running, screaming, beating, burning, shooting.
Helicopter rescues and taxi chases.
All the usual.

The fictions do not seem very different
from the facts that words and images convey.
Best not keep it hidden? My opinion
changes. Maybe. So they say.

AUTUMN GARDEN POEM

---

i
I want to know the name of those leaves,
pale and felted one side
smooth and green

the other, like strips of paper torn
from an endless scroll and strewn
across the lawn.

45

ii
Two Japanese ladies, leaning
fondly as lovers: a willow's
ragged sleeves

brushing the grass. The jade-blue discs
silvered by dew and frost
from a eucalyptus

bush are their broken necklaces.
Spiders' webs have tangled
their lank tresses.

iii
I can show you rosebay and golden
rod, moulting thistles
and rusty clover.

But what are those pallid flowers called
that open in sunlight and close
when the evening falls?

Stuart Henson

GIRL WITH A CAT

(after the painting by Pierre-Auguste Renoir, 1880)

It is morning in the *Rue Cortot*,
warm morning; the sunlight crumbles the walls
like bread and the dust falls
in the window's eye and delights
with its touch the surface of things.
There are bees in the garden,
the dew is gone. A grey dappled cat
lies asleep in a quoin of the roof
and below in the courtyard
an old woman sings.

Angèle, how you prattle – of nothing,
of lives, of the warmth of the sun,
but you can't sit still
and your dark lids droop
and the picture that *Monsieur Renoir*
has begun is nothing – no good.
You are young; you must sleep
you have love on your side
and your pert young face is your fortune
though not for long.

In the courtyard the woman is feeding the cat;
it curls round her feet with its fur
like smoke. It purrs and it arches
and dips at the milk. The painter leans out
with his hands on the sill. The garden
is full of the light of poppies and daisies,
shade-alleys of grasses and speechless leaves . . .

47

but the frame of the window
is suddenly empty – Renoir is descending
the staircase in leaps.

She is young; she must sleep;
her heart's hopes are simple; her face is her fortune
though not for long. And *Monsieur Renoir*
has begun again in his *grande affaire*
with the surface of things.
It is morning in the *Rue Cortot*,
warm morning; from the courtyard below
the smell of bread baking.
The cat shuts its eyes in the street-girl's lap
and the painter smiles and his brushes sing.

Michael Hofmann

UP IN THE AIR

The sky was breaking, and I felt little less numb
than the alcoholic devotedly spooning
pâté from a tub; than the divorcee's station wagon
with its dog-haired sheepskin dogseat;
or the birds barking in the trees to greet the day . . .

There was a grey heron standing on a green bank.
'Soul survivors' spilled out of the *Titanic*
in their once-fluorescent sailing whites.
You only live once. The record sang 'My Girl',
but that was a lie. She only shucked my cigarette packet,

as she danced before my eyes like the alphabet,
mostly like the letter A . . . I was Ajax,
I had stolen another man's captive, slaughtered sheep
like a maniac, counted my friends till
I fell asleep, now I would have to swim for it

in the greasy, yellow, woollen waves . . .
The bass drum went like a heart, there was a pillow
curled in the bottom of it for anchorage.
Our finger-joints shook in the free air,
sheep's knuckle-bones dicing for the seamless garment.

Three hours flat out on the hotel candlewick,
blunting my creases, then off to the airport
with its complement of tiny, specialized, ministering
vehicles. I sat over the wing, riveted, wary,
remembering ring fingers and flying kites.

THE LATE RICHARD DADD, 1817–1886

The *Kentish Independent* of 1843
carried his pictures of his father, himself
and the scene of his crime. The first photo-journalist:
fairy-painter, father-slayer, poor, bad, mad Richard Dadd.

His extended Grand Tour took in the Holy Land
and ended in Bethlem Hospital, with its long, panoptical
galleries, spider-plants, whippets and double-gaslights.
He had outlived himself at twenty-six . . .

There was one day he seemed to catch sunstroke.
He fancied the black, scorched beard of a sheikh
would furnish him with some 'capital paintbrushes'.
Sailing up the Nile, on the *Hecate*,

they spent Christmas Day eating boiled eggs
and plum pudding, and playing cards for the captain's soul.
The temples at Luxor stood under a full moon, lightly
    boiled.
Sir Thomas got off to try and bag a crocodile.

The route up from Marseille went as the crow flies –
precipitately, a dash from ear to ear.
A fellow-traveller let him play with his collar and tie,
until he pulled out 'an excellent English razor'.

There was his watercolour, 'Dead Camel',
and a series of drawings of his friends,
all with their throats cut,
Frith, Egg, Dadd, Phillip and O'Neill.

He saw himself as a catspaw, Osiris's right hand man
on earth. His digs in Newman Street
contained three hundred eggs, and the earth
cracked when he walked on it.

Donald Hope

APRIL IN HARLEY STREET

Still as the sick-room flowers, with a fixed stare
from hollow eyes, as blank as glass, at air,
she lay for three whole days and nights, half propped
up on her pillows – her thick glasses dropped
down beak-thin slope of nose, rings loosely rolled
round stick-thin fingers – waiting to go cold;
till her last long-drawn-out rattling gale of breath
shook her to a mere husk, sucked dry by death.
We stare, as if to feed our memory
on the last scraps of sight – sharp, white and grey
ridges and folds of sheet and skin and bone.
Shrunk like a garment and silent as stone,
she lies there, and not there. Thought can't take hold
on that frail glacier-face; the mind slips, chilled.
We go, leaving her to the undertaker
in his black coat; now it's his job to make a
last, neat arrangement of her, for the fire.
Out in the street, as the spring sun climbs higher,
light licks down the grey walls, and flowers blaze
in window-boxes, through the lengthening days.
My widowed father, my two brothers, me –
we stand together at the curb and see
the flash of metal as the cars go by;
then part in three directions – I to my
wife at home waiting for me. We'll all meet
again tomorrow; meanwhile I talk, eat,
try to work, even laugh, being alive
for now – and in no hurry to arrive
at the brick building with the long black drive
and the big chimney, where what's left of Mother
will soon go up in smoke – into that other

world she half hoped for, maybe, if it's there;
or, I think, into ashes and thin air.

MONEY

(Variation on a theme of Philip Larkin)

Monthly, it is, money reproaches me
in columns of printed figures, marked OD
in capital letters in the margin – 'Why
do you spend so much too much? Why don't you try
to make more of me? Why don't you stop and think
what you're doing, and have some sense? Why do you
    drink?'

And I think of my children, and hard-working wife,
and our two houses, and car, and the good life
we ought to be living; and my useless work,
that often I don't even do, but shirk.
And the little black numbers swarm across the page,
and seeing them fills me with black shame and rage.

I listen to money nagging and complaining:
it's like looking out of the window when it's raining,
and seeing the brilliant world go dull and grey
and people huddled up, hurrying away
in all directions. And I tell myself
how lucky I am, having so much pelf
as I do have – and what a crashing bore
thinking of money is – and long for more.

Michael Horovitz

GOTHIC EVANESCENCE

What spiked and grisly clanking of chains
   throughout the night
whose god spills a watering-can of moonbeams
splayed across moats and dungeons crammed brimful
with ruthlessly grated limbs, rotting
coffins of ashes of once young lovers'
cunts cocks balls breasts arses mouldering oblivious . . . to

what slimy inroads of reptilian amours and excrescence,
of vultures –   tarantulas –   pterodactyls
  circling . . . closing . . . roiling . . .

whilst savage amplified crow-calls and rook KRRAAAKs
flood chock the ears of a damsel shackled in the bell tower
of this highwalled bayonet-battlemented clifftop garage?

Her tears cascade to rills that well about her sandalled feet
above the ankles now, but her cruel guardians,
the firefanged tank-hooved centaurs, only cackle and screech
at her discomfiture
               ∠ till
on sudden, all these sounds and agencies
of torture and encroachment falter, then dissolve
as the heart of darkness fades
beneath a muslin . . . soft furnishings of day
with steady spurts of chirrupy birdage,
delivery vans, good egg –   milkfloats,
cleaners, papers   – the ordinary alarums
of ground control
that monitor, and electricly dismiss
the incipient terrorists called
                  our dreams.

T.C. Hudson

JOHN RUSKIN REVIVIFIED

Saint Ursula asleep – precisely plied
his brushes limn Carpaccio's
design – facsimiled to soothe
his outraged nerves – a ploy
to quell the anguish of his loss.
Saint Ursula – the 'little bear' –
the strange conceit evokes, against
his mood, a smile – and then, as if
the Cornish maid, once martyred in
Cologne, so willed, he sees with
unscaled eyes the wild verbena –
dianthus sees, dissociate from Zeus –
the twain a symbol sent to purge
the scepticism from his soul.
Saint Ursula – her Christmas gift
dispensed, lies dreaming still, while he
accepts the miracle – allows
the spike-leaved vervain's magic to
renew his faith – nor questions if
some self-deception work inside
his tortured mind.
Aglow with hope: convinced a link
between the revelation and
his Irish Rose obtains, he lets
supernal guidance take command –
determines henceforth to obey
its sacred call.
Atonement made, he goes with joy,
with quasi-ecstasy, to bed;
while, sanctified, his youthful Rose,
ensepulchred, lies two years dead.

Peter Hughes

GIFT WRAPPING

that pot plant didn't last long

stranded on its reflections
in the glass table like a drowned trick

its little claw of roots
wouldn't keep a dandelion
in the manner to which it's accustomed

so instead I give you that tree
outside the window by the river

although I don't know to what extent it's mine

or to what extent it could be yours

you don't bring it in in Winter
its roots go under the road

you don't water it in Summer
its roots go into the river

you don't keep it
from the direct rays of the sun

its branches dress the light that wakes us

Nicki Jackowska

GORPLE

for David

And we returned to the four-square page
again, again, where the journey is begotten.
I am not well armed having cut spinach
last week and picked these few chicken bones.
But you, ambitious, want the whole
Titanic up, and all its populations.
Yet I am told by years and expeditions
it is not wisdom to restore the wreck.

And we fall back into the four-square bed
and close ranks, and I must visit, touch
the bald rock's slant, feel where its tilt
might tumble me, hear the wind beyond you
and each love's impudence; yet it is not that
it was not like that, we did not speak
of this, only set it loose among our flesh
and grasses, lean easy at the gaunt rock's grip.

MOONSHOT

Reaching out to trespass on that ice-sheet
where you are not; only the moon-light
spreading fins across me, and where
should looking end if I go out

56

and tramp the lawn's mud down
at night, when you have peeled away
your selves and curled alone upstairs
or in the hollow of a northern hill.

What then I sing alone will call
the moonlight in and rocking over all
the bed, heat it where you are not
and dance alone for all the world's light.
Bare feet on an untreated lawn, seeding
it late, the grass unruly, tufted.
I crouch and moan under these dead trees
and hope for lightning, roar from the sky.

This morning's catalogue inches its nifty
t-shirts round my skin, a subtle moon-shade
in the knit; going out was just to
catch the edge of where I am not.
Now the silk flood of a clever shirt
pulls down torrents, she clutches at his
saxophone wearing white spots; my fingers
ply the page, try last night on for size.

Alan Jenkins

BIOGRAPHER

For this, our final heart-to-heart
you meet me in a room by the sea,
the floor almost underwater,
a single kerosene lamp.

As we step outside, the salt spray
stings our eyes. You say,
I dreamt the war was still going on.
The whole thing makes me so damn tired . . .

You decide to make a run for the border
from where you will travel steerage on a tramp
for Madagascar, but fetch up in Marseille.
Papers, for once, in order.

As always, there is the part
I'll need to rewrite,
your saying you wished you could be left alone,
the rest drowned by surf slapping at the wall.

Last seen in a bar
on the Canebière
by now you might be anywhere,
if you are anywhere at all.

THE PROMISE

Your 'just getting hold of a boat
and going off' was always a possibility,
though each year it looked more remote.
They're still there, waiting: the jetty
and an M.F.V., and the inn,
all weatherboard and varnish, high stools
ranged along the bar – *The Spanish Main*,
I've seen it – waiting too. Our rooms would have
that smoke-and-whisky smell, a masculine
perfection. We'd never shave
closer than a quarter-inch of stubble, you'd perform
your favourite role, the Outcast of the Islands,
mad for rum and mescalin.
And the only real ship of fools
would bring them from Miami for the season,
paying to the hilt to chase marlin,
bewildered by our surly silence.
At night we'd be running firearms
to Cuba or Jamaica, lashing down tarpaulin,
taking money for old rope in the Keys –
you'd keep your knack of riding out the storms.

WINTERING

Flushed, unfussed, unreluctant, dapper,
you masterminded the bonfire, the Guy, the catherine
    wheels.
I came trotting at your gum-booted heels
when you strode up to light the blue touch-paper
and stood clear, suddenly a silhouette
drawing on the umpteenth cigarette.

Or you'd hang around in your duffle-coat
being one of the boys, diffident
and smiling, buying rounds from a pub that didn't close
all night, while I stamped and froze
and clutched a hot-dog, a cup of soup,
watching the Regent Street lights go up.

It was snow you hated most, and there was snow
the day of your funeral; and a week or so
after, the neighbours had a mass said for you
though you hated all religions too –
snow on the church, the crib, the shepherds and kings,
like a blueprint I found among your things.

Three years ago, the first time, I got away –
a cottage on an estuary, some friends, some booze.
Someone took a photograph of my back –
sky, mud-flats and shoreline are the same grey
and I'm wearing duffle-coat and boots,
looking out, scenting tar, salt, seaweed and wrack.

Anne Jones

WORD AFFAIR

Words began it
words joined us together
yours confident, polished, published,
mine confused, parochial, pardonable,
continued close continued distanced
holding words whispered words
hot slightly obscene words
words moulded re-moulded
thoughtless words mirrored words
such careful un-careful words
regretful words kind yet firm words
loud soft sad cooling cold frozen words
no words.

Sylvia Kantaris

COUPLE, PROBABLY ADULTEROUS

(Assen, Holland, *circa* Roman times)

Just another couple of old lovers dragged up
from a bog and propped behind glass, cured,
their faces slipping off, their ribs skew-whiff.
Note her split crotch and the scroll of skin teased
stiff between his legs. A joke? ('You know the one
about this bloke called Tristan and some other
joker's missus?') It's a laugh a minute
getting it together in black leather after death,
even for monogamists. What price Rapunzel
and the prince, her switch of rusted hair now quite
detached from what's left of her cranium? Old rope!
He falls into the thicket of his sockets.

'They leave me cold,' my friend says, moving on
to look at moths or something. I'm still
fascinated, like a necrophiliac.
(Two reflections meet in the showcase,
shrug and pass – young lovers.) I move in
and concentrate on coupled carcasses
preserved beyond the grave like sacred relics
run to puffball dust. They ought to be released.
(I won't come back. You smothered love with guilt.
Now picture us light-heartedly united
in the afterlife as in this sad museum
of the sporty risen. It's a sick joke.)

'Well?' (I jump.) My friend consults his watch:
'Everything's been said about bog people. Aren't

you bored?' I shrug, agree they also leave me cold.
(As if I'd passed over my grave.) 'And yet,'
he says, 'such lifelike fingernails?' Shiftily,
I hide my ten quick half-moons, and concentrate
religiously on dead black imitations. Yes,
I've nothing new to say; we know how words
embalm us in old habits. 'Still, I'd like
to buy a postcard for an old acquaintance.'
We sift through all the pictures – swords and moths.
Late season; adulterers are out of stock.

Roy Kelly

FOREIGN EXCHANGES

Perhaps Heaven is like being foreign abroad
where even groceries appear exotic.
Strange and familiar the language excludes you
though apparently all is recognizable,
everything is happening before your eyes.
Look. That family at the restaurant table.
The baby's busy grasping fingers. The father's
evident pleasure in the touch of wife and child.
All is before you exactly as it seems.
Everything is as false and true as dreams.

The money looks like works of art, pastel-coloured,
microscopically detailed with engravings
of cross-hatched curlicues, the figures denoting
value grown abstract and meaningless with beauty,
these portraits of dead statesmen finally useful.
The beautiful money changes hands once again.
The baby is smeared with chocolate ice cream.
His tender parents are watchful before the lake.
Yet you feel larger meaning eluding you.
Relax on these caféd squares. Inspect the view.

A morning haze that promises to last the day
blends the mountain silhouettes, the sky and the lake
in smoky greys and blue variations on blue.
Earth and water seem as insubstantial as clouds.
Climb the hills behind the town. (There are always hills
behind the town.) Walk the painful cobble footpaths.
The baby's mouth and fingers are being wiped clean.
His parents are preparing him for travelling.
Stop and catch your breath. Up here in the hills
terracotted geraniums crowd the sills.

Along the terraces the precarious farms,
smallholdings, and outbuildings all seem deserted,
except for skinny cats and large patrolling dogs.
One remembers that they too speak another tongue.
The cockerels look as our cockerels do:
the peculiar headflesh tumescently red.
The baby is far below them, along the shore,
dozing on his way from one meal to another.
Tiny lizards skitter the encrusted walls,
disturbed tasting the air where warm sunlight falls.

And now the lake is furrowed with the long white wakes
of steamers and ferries, clear despite the haze.
A silent pale triangular sail tacks its way
to a blurred destination. The car ferry hoots.
You are learning to call things by another name.
All external appearance may be like this.
The baby is fractious or sound asleep. Half-light
filters through the high corridors of old hotels.
Look, your artistic banknote promises bliss.
Perhaps visiting your Heaven is like this.

James Kirkup

BREAKDANCERS IN WEST BERLIN

On the Ku-damm, outside Wertheim's closed for
    Christmas,
in the rainy late afternoon, they are all here again,
the seven youths with their ghetto-blasters,
in worn-out jeans and T-shirts, but brand-new sneakers –
Adidas, Puma, Nike Golf – for it is the feet
that make or break a body-popping breakdancer.

It helps, too, to have a boneless body
that can creep on air like serpent or caterpillar.
Each boy a Valentin le Désossé without knowing it,
doing the zombie strut, the comicbook freeze on liquid legs,
electric boogie robot rap with rippling spine
and fluid arms in transit music doing the Thing,
the level head keeping its chin just above imagined water
in a controlled glide that makes the earth appear to move
under effortless soles, a moving walkway, while the canted
    torso
swings upright like a seahorse on human hooves
hugging the ocean bed of night's bleak pavements
outside Wertheim's on the Ku-damm, closed for Christmas.

This group is called the Zoo Scratchers – their usual pitch
at the Kaiser Wilhelm Gedächtniskirche taken over by
the Weihnachtsmarkt shooting galleries and dodgems.
They take it in turns to solo – each with his own
performing style, a deft routine, original and witty,
practised, always unexpected, comical and grave –
they take this streetdance very seriously, however easy
they make it look. Such concentration makes them move
like spacemen or delicately-programmed Petrushkas
round the growing ring of rapt spectators.

At the end of each brief virtuoso turn
they pass round a beat-up baseball cap
for a few small coins, to keep them in sneakers –
they wear out two pairs a week, such is their intensity
and dedication to their art, all for our passing, casual
    entertainment,
but also for their own total release from everyday horror –
from frustration, unemployment, poverty, despair,
from the Wall's illegible graffiti, from perishing Pershings,
these cast-offs of the affluent democracy – lost children
of Gastarbeiter, Turks, Arabs, Greeks, Yugoslavs and
    blacks –
they find a kind of peace at last, new strength, and pride
in their agility, their backbreaking handstand flip-flops,
young bodies pulsing pure energy, power no factory can use,
in rhythm to the riffs of maniacal drummers
that no mass-production line can cope with.
(Who wants a workman who can head-spin pirouette?)
'It's only aliens like us can kick the breaks,'
they rap, street-wise. 'These homegrown Prussian kids
are too uptight, they can't let go and risk their necks.'

Let go these outsiders do, and with complete abandon,
    careless
of opinion, intent only on their own interpretations of
a state of mind that says Fuck 1984, a funky far-out beat
some call eccentric, or at best perverse. Next morning,
they are gone till nightfall comes again, so do not see
dawn workmen chopping down with dripping axes in the
    rain
Wertheim's genuine Christmas trees, for the New Year
    sales.

Stephen Knight

ON THE EDGE OF MONDAY MORNING

Against the wall, like a square of chocolate,

The storage heater snores through the small hours:

Heat blossoms from every pore, curling round

The tendrils of the television set.

Two storeys up, the potted plants look out

Of place. Last night is melting on the pane.

In the broad-leafed shadows, my mother wakes.

Five blind fingers go feeling for the clock.

WHEN THE SUMMER GOES UP IN FLAMES

Men smoke two storeys above your parting,
Capitalizing on the sunshine –
Brick and slate take root in the garden.
The landlord pops in with his landscaped,
Baldy hairstyle and we complain about
The noise. Skips become a fitment.

To those events of 1986
Recognized in Special Issue stamps

68

– Halley's comet, the Commonwealth Games –
We add the growing row over sanctions
And the tufts of grass on your back.

The grass on your back and buttocks tickles
In bed, as we weigh the pros and cons
For scorching. (Zico shimmers through Poles
In the heat of Guadalajara:
A shadow of his former self, he vies
For air-time with Desmond Tutu.)

During downpours, of course, you rush inside
And watch the box; men rattle the planks
Above us: *we* try horticulture.
When, arms outstretched at night, the spiders come
To you, scorching crops up again.

Pulling a single blade across my lips,
Between my teeth, burns the skin. Despite
A speech impediment, I'm whingeing
About your chlorophyll – it messes
The sheets. When I roam the length of your spine,
Green tongues leap between my fingers.

Down among the rubble, the sun that cooks
My shoulders salmon-pink turns your field
To gold. Still tender, you embrace me
Gingerly: I slip through your flattened palms
Like a fish damp with calamine.

The scaffolding goes and I catch myself
Staring at my empty hands, missing
Ladders and pulleys; the languorous,
Autumnal drift of paper falling
To the garden; and talk, idle talk – that
Most peculiar of vapours.

Lotte Kramer

THEFT

This summer was the shortest I remember,
That season's paucity prepares no winter.

So we complain until we read about
That chimney sweep who stands in Leningrad,

A shadow of himself, a scientist
Whose words hardly accuse, only explain:

'I know now that they've stolen my life.'
There is no summer in his strangled year.

AT WEISSENSEE, morning

I
A storm in the night left meadow and wood
Sodden as washing. Clouds are settled
Featherbeds. Yesterday a rabbit dead
And stretched white on a soft hill. Flies fed

On his fur. We stared and questioned. No blood.
His brown companion hopping about him
A funeral rite, perplexed. We saw sad
Lines on his flapping face. Or a whim

Of our fancy, perhaps. Today no corpse
But wild mint profuse at the waterfall,

Strong scent among flowers and raindrops
As we goose-stepped our way along the wall

Of sheerness. Then in the forest the path
Knotted with roots. No slippery aftermath.

Maureen Guyan Lalor

FATHER

It was a form of worship, I suppose.
A seeking of perfection,
An act of re-creation
For the week that lay ahead.

Coming home from Sunday School,
On wintery days we'd find you
With a paper spread across your lap,
Your left hand buried deep inside a shoe,
Your right hand index finger wrapped in cloth
And tracing circles on the leather toe,
Erasing every scratch and scuff.

The air was pungent with the polish smell.
Around you all the shoes that we possessed
Would look as if they meant to board the Ark,
All neat and shining, ranked across the floor.
Your zeal would batten on the shoes we wore,
And they would join the others without flaw,
Condemning us to stay indoors
Through long, dull, Sabbath winter afternoons,
Odours of cleanliness pervading every room.

John Latham

EXORCIST

On each one of the years of nights since then
– when he forced himself from coma,
stared around the room, milk-blind,
failed to find us, strained
until he snapped back, dead –
I've squeezed my eyes, willed him into view.
He's come reluctantly, distorted, never whole:
a fragment of his forehead, an elongated chin,
a mocking grin he never had, loose-cobwebbed eyes.
In those thousand nights, he never smiled.

Perhaps it was your fingers' music as we talked,
or seeds gliding all ways past our window: today,
strangers, we shaped a vision, shared it
– a bubble, floating, sloughing violet and green,
a ladybird inside it, swollen by the lens,
sliding down a curved slope – trapped;
the bubble wobbling in the slip-stream of a wing,
bursting in a cataract of stars;
a red bead lifting, swirling off.
Your smile was from inside the bubble.

Tonight he was lying in a field, intact,
face open to the sun, which chased a ladybird
deep into the caverns of his hair
– now brown again.
He rocked on to his elbow, and as he smiled at me
his fingers traced the full length of a straw,
lingered at a knot,
untying it. He smoothed its creases out,
tucked it in the grass.
For a moment, his smile, huge above my cot.

A fifty-year-old knot that couldn't be undone
until you floated diffidently in,
my exorcist,
and for an hour, in mottled space,
from half-dreams and our ignorance
we shaped a fugue and pared it.
I never touched your fingers,
and now his smile has gone
I can find only fragments of your face.
His darkness is completed: I can sleep.

AS I LIE DYING

We skirt the Vistula, piggy-back tired tumbleweed
in Yoknapatawpha County, inhale the smell of words
and whelks in old O'Connell Street, slink along
St Petersburg's stone flags. My face is brushed
by Sonya's fingers, I breathe her sackcloth hair,
but Lebedyev is tugging me, her glove flies free,
she recoils into a doorway, and on the lantern's
faint horizon she is swallowed by the damp cloak
of a pock-marked general. At an upstairs window,
Pierre, in heavy spectacles, wrestles with a bear.

A month at most, the doctor said. The bookshelves
in my drifting head are crammed. No space to make
new friends – a time for family: they stir, begin
to mill. I flounder through my fever, but the wind
has veered again, mist hissing, curtaining my eyes.

Tressilian, straw-sandalled, stiffly at the door:
a large room, vague with smoke and muted laughter,
Mrs Gamp and Lebedyev careering round with trays.
Vardaman spills mead on Mr Knightley, hypnotised
by Catherine's white whip. The quartet strikes up:
Maggie Tulliver's drowned toes paddling ballads
in bowls of shallow water, Huck rocking his barrel
to the plaint of Castorp's punctured throat, Flay
dictating tempo with the cracking of his knees,

echoing from conch-shells on the onyx chandeliers.

Outside, those great unread, whom I am spurning:
not a burning of the books, just an abandonment
to fresher libraries. My friends gather, populate
the shifting dark with movement, voice and shade.
How disorderly they are: how blurred and intimate.

Tull whirrups the mule along the Nevsky Prospect,
pawns Nastasya Filippovna, sheathed in concrete,
ankles turning green. 'Now I can git them teeth,'
Prince Myshkin cries. A small boy sucks a mirror,
a clown weeps in his bath. Molly swirls her skirts
around Giles Winterborne: Oskar is soft-drumming
underneath with K. Sonya beckons from the shadows
of an alley, her hand thinned almost to the bone.
Where our wrist-skins touch it burns with fever.
But Lebedyev is tugging at me – tugging very hard.

LATITUDE OR LONGITUDE

They take up little space – grandfather, brother, father –
together on your shelf:
your fingers stroke them – vellum, paper, cloth.

You kneel, raise him, leaf by brittle leaf,
his certificates, long-hand,
from university in Riga: the Emperor's seal, cracked wax.

You translate slowly – lingering with the whorls,
loops, mottled curlicues –
coax him from the box: not the trim white-bearded man

who tossed you in the air, tramped fields with you,
but a smooth-cheeked youth
huddled on a boat: shivering, trying to strain west.

The mist through which you see him mutes his colours,
subdues the texture of his voice,

the way he shaped stories with eyebrows, chin, squat hands

– the same, I think as those resting on the box
as you blow old dust away, say
'If *he* could open these he'd be engulfed in visions.'

Uncomfortable here, thinned by a century's erosion,
would his awakening be easier
riding time's contours, across a shorter stretch of sea,

to a sunken cottage at the end of a dirt lane,
where a man who couldn't read
who has my gait, shoulders, my brother's quiet grace,

leans forwards, stabbing coals in the middle of the night,
watching sparks curl and shoot away,
while his wife lies cooling in their marriage bed,

and three children, underneath the garret's thatch
– one already with my father's eyes –
toss and burble, sleep their last mother-filled sleep?

As your fingers delve, trace his scores in algebra,
air trapped in Odessa
floats out of your window towards Puget Sound.

It is time to put the box away. Perhaps, in twenty years,
a fourth book will join the others
on the shelves of a man who frowns like you – or him.

The fog will have thickened. And it should be enough
to listen for the whisper of a scuffle,
which might be boots on planking – or a poker in the ash.

Sarah Lawson

THOSE CRUTCHES

I take your elbow crutches
To put in the back seat
But they catch on things
Like a pair of coathangers.
I hold them in one hand, giant chopsticks
I could pick up the dog with.
They splay out and resist passively
As though I'm trying to arrest them.
Finally I use both hands and they behave
And I wonder what your trick is.
Using them must be a stunt
Like not falling off a pair of stilts.

We sit equal in our wheelchair,
All metal and motorized, and no one sees
The pair of sticks stowed in back –
Those ski poles to use without the skis.

Robin Leanse

ON REMBRANDT'S PORTRAIT OF HIS SON TITUS

Half-shade; a dark carved square;
a father's tribulation on the eyes;
he sits and paints his son. The paint glows. Love
drives the unerring brush, love quotes the care:
my son is sad, like art, at one remove.
Like art? the painting finished, standing there,
was it his son's grief, or was it his own,
this resignation in the child's straight eyes?
his father could draw, paint, engrave in stone,
but not stop mother's asthma, or her death,
and not change pain, the shock when something dies
into a sign of pain, with its own breath . . .
does painting help the heart to recognize
just how much pain there is in human love?
In Rembrandt's genius I could see how life
overflowed like a bowl of bitter fruits
whose beauty came from hints of death; but how
to tell if such great works transcend the grief
they paint so purely? Death pulled man from wife
and child from mother. Death pulls from the roots
its last word – incarnation – tugging now.
And so is grief to die or not to die?
It's beautiful, it's painful, makes you cry.
But suddenly I'm happy to be here –
it's as if what to recognize at last
is not at all transcendence, but relief
to feel what can't be changed so very near;
my death brings something running from the past
wanting to take this too. It's life. The thief
whose swag is happiness, relief, and grief.

MOVING

i

Getting a house; with money that's not hard;
but just in case the money came too easy
this cheque's too large to back with Barclaycard
and what's to pay's not money but more sleasy –
for you the price is tax-exile in Gib.
Did dad mean you to stay there all your life
– you ask, and weep; tears laundering the fib
he coined of 'Home Sweet Home' – for me, my wife
and little Tom. Back 'home' you'd come to see it,
not yet bought, quite a mess inside – and talked
of how six years on's done no good, albeit
now you've stuck the lot in Trust for us.
Outside the house I wanted as we walked
it had to be you, homeless, we'd discuss.

ii

But what I think of's how you beat self-pity,
(I needed shaking out of mine for you)
you broke off suddenly with 'Look, that's pretty . . .!'
the bush you'd pointed at, not one I knew,
was full of creamy groups of spray-shaped flowers
just opening in July. Well, did I know it?
The front wall it hung over wasn't 'Ours' –
it took our minds off exile, though. I'll grow it –
the first thing I'll plant, if I get my way,
in that long south-west facing garden Mum.
I don't care what the books on flowers say,
that bush's name is In Memoriam
the Home Sweet Home it stopped you weeping for.
One tear-jerker to snap me out of more.

iii

It moves me, and it isn't just aesthetic,
that help's what beauty's for: you showed it best,
latching on like a baby to the breast –
to something 'pretty'. Poetry's pathetic,

79

I never help you, mum, like you help me.
It's money talks, it's never poetry.
But if that day you'd phoned to say how money'd
messed up our lives, how once we'd been so close,
I'd had the bravery to write this sonnet
perhaps you'd have, well not quite said 'That's pretty'
but latched on to my Mother's Ruin dose . . .
and helped to move me from my poet's slum . . .
from where the lucre's filthy in the kitty
and lucre says 'This poet exploits mum.'

Keith Lindsay

MAINLAND

'Ye canna die yet,' laughed the ferryman,
'I have'ne polished the oars.'
But she did.
They wound her in the black dress
that had only seen Sundays,
And smoothed her out, cold, in the kitchen.

As is their custom
each croft gave a clapboard
John made the box
for the ferrying home.

When, later, the oars were polished
they pulled her to the mainland,
to the graveyard of the old gods,
and lowered her softly
to the sound of the gaelic.
The bell called the passing
and the women's shawls
shifted from shoulders to heads.

Adam Lively

GROUND BENEATH, WATER OVERHEAD

When I was young we used to play a game
Of walking bold across the ocean bed.
The skill lay in gripping the ground beneath
And advancing to increase the volume of water
Overhead. He or she who floated
Or lost her breath came in last.
Why not play a game of follow-my-leader?
We could walk together in single file
Like a column of soldiers, to China or beyond.
We'll follow the curves of the ocean floor
Together. Only one of us must lead.
One of us must dip his head beneath
The surface. Only we really will follow,
Like walking in our sleep, into the green water.
Only it must be a slow march.
We must each feel our hair floating on the surface
As our faces grow used to the wetness ahead.
We have already gone. We have already made that walk.
In dreams we've seen ourselves erect in the shifting tide
And treading ground that feet have never touched before.

Roy MacGregor-Hastie

NEW CRITICISM

'Who told you to paint Germans and buffoons?'

Art critics always like to have the last word –
the first, too, if they can.
$\qquad$ Paolo Veronese soon
found out what he had done wrong. Standing, he heard
the three Inquisitors in the chapel of St Theodore:
'Who told you to paint St Peter carving a lamb?'
Veronese, at some risk, seemed to ask for more
when he pointed out the Last Supper was a meal. The jamb
probably had lambs' blood on it. It was Passover, after all.
He hoped the Fathers had noticed the toothpick in the hand
of one of the disciples. Were there toothpicks, then?
$\qquad$ Paul
was painted by Carpaccio with a toothpick, and a band
playing him on.
$\qquad$ 'And what about the dog in the foreground?'
Did the Venetian Inquisitors hate dogs? In a way, so do I
especially in smart streets where dogs fed on pork pie
seem to excrete, exquisitely, turds the colour of crust.
Back to the Inquisition, which said that Veronese must
paint out the dog and put in the Magdalen instead,
even though the painting was for the refectory of 'red'
Saints John and Paul, their Dominican Church. Again:
'Does it seem proper to you to surround the Table of Our
$\quad$ Lord
with dogs and drunkards, Germans, buffoons, dwarfs in
$\quad$ pain,
not to speak of toothpicking disciples and other frauds?'
I have always thought that Veronese got it absolutely right,
down to the detail of the lamb, not beef or pork, of course.

But clerks are always set over us to put their honest blight
– that camel drafting council went on to criticize the horse
So what's the use?
                              For Veronese, being shrewd the way out
                                   was easy
He just went home and changed the title to Feast in the
     House of Levi.

Mairi MacInnes

THE CAVE-IN

What did he say, that blinded dusty boy,
when he was dug out? – That at first the darkness
of the cave-in lay identical, outside and in,
across his eyelids; that the cries
he shrilled met stone and cried back to him
as echoes. He was imprisoned by an entire hill.
So humble and colossal it was, he cried until
the cold stationed in his boots wormed up
to his armpits, and threaded itself on vertebrae
and folded round his belly in a web.
So his tears dried up in convulsive shivers;
the taste of salt and tannin dried out his head.

When he came to, he heard thumps –
his heart, perhaps, or a pavement tamper,
and increasingly nearer, a flutter of water,
a streaming, pounding, a clatter of hooves
that halted almost on top of him. He knew the advance
of a heavy animal, he smelled sweet grass
on its breath, and acrid hairiness of hide,
before he felt on his ears the bloom
of huge warm lips, tenderly, curiously applied,
and the nudge of damp nostrils on his neck,
and recognized the pushiness of a great beast
used to its own success.

        He got up (he said)
oh, joyfully, and touched the warm and rounded moleskin
of the side, which shut in tons of brilliant flesh,
and felt it glide under his hands, and twitch, ticklish,
till in a gigantic snatch it bolted off

slap into the rock, and there the skull and skeleton
sparked like a lode, or a luminous fossil,
the bones of a horse running; while he heard,
a good way off, the noise of hooves.

What a horse was doing there, what it meant,
he'd no time to wonder before the rescuers
broke through the rockfall and found him.

Ruth Morse

ADVICE

Wherever we turn, we're up against the ambiguity in all
tragedy: that death is both the punishment of the evil and
the reward of the vituous, besides being the same end for
everybody.

Northrop Frye

No one had told me what to expect,
though they promised – or so it seemed –
I'd understand when I got there
or there simply arrived.

Everyone told me exactly what to expect,
an allegorical journey to get wisdom.
I can't say I wasn't tricked
out, I didn't prepare.
I was game.

No one said how much you have to endure
and only one that middle age
would be largely a matter of
not losing your nerve.

Every year I go on beating the bounds
uncertain if I remember the way.
Between me and my storybook friends
lies this: I know I am in a tale.

No one told me this is what to expect,
frustration of effort, all this to do,
beating through seas of air,

that deliverance is all you
get there.

GAMBIT

'On my last visit to the chess club
I was displaced. The predictable
kid put paid to my dreams with a thud.'

Why is this anecdotal boy *twelve*
in all stories of defeat at chess?
Perhaps because he is free of sex,

free of distraction from anything
newfound but passion. Perhaps that's it.
In these stories something else is hid,

something to do with our departure
from his childhood's frangible border,
one-way membrane. Briefly, the parterre

is empty, the curtain on the point
of rising, ditto the sap, the coils
of spring, all our retrospective joy.
Hunkering, inevitable boy!

Christina Muirhead

POLISH PRISMS

Your wife is alone in the hotel garden,
she sits impassive in a gaily striped deckchair
neatly centred in the square of cut grass.
The air is still as an interrogation room
before the terror begins. She has closed
her hands and sealed her eyes and lips
clutching in the hurt, but it seeps and shouts
through every pore. Even her Polish moon-face
betrays her raped soul.

Down among the vegetables your brother works
slowly, without love of soil.
His sleeves rolled up exposing thick white
arms extending to stubby fingers, frustrated
by their lack of greenness. He is more at home
in the kitchen using his meat cleaver,
mumbling incorrect staccato English as he takes
orders from the dining room. Stuttering
to a stubborn silence of deliberate misunderstandings.
Have they butchered his mind to match his
butcher's body?

And you, have sandpapered yourself
to a smooth-talking hotel proprietor
with coat upon coat of polished façade,
so that the world slips-off on contact.
Even your accent is bland as tap water.
So why do I catch you staring, with ice-hot
eyes, melting the thin cotton blouse
I have on, until it is I who feel the invaded.

Paul Munden

GREETINGS CARDS

The old masters, untucked
from their little envelopes
are ranged on the mantel.
Those obviously missing
are crossed off in the book.

Mine are all hand-made
and still the news is brief
to cryptic. Between the lines
the swelling sentiment –
don't go out of my life.

THE ATTIC

---

is not part of his workaday house.
It took the junk, then one Christmas
a railway – double 0 gauge – for his son
who showed no interest. The track, tacked
to chipboard climbs to an eggbox tunnel;
modelling, washed a rural green. He moves
the porters, engineers about their business
just as he pleases. His little boy sparked
at a war scenario: in with the Afrika Korps,
the Eighth Army in shorts – matt khaki
and a very pink *flesh* you could believe
was skin, blistered by the desert sun.
Since then Dad's made do without people

in his scrupulous landscape, happier
with rolling stock – how the couplings
latch; the electric signal gantry. Trains
are driven at a purr. This way he abides
the scream, the massive clank and roar,
the distorting public address, the abuse.
Some think he's not all there up top.

Ruth Padel

AMNIOCENTESIS

Linea nigra, my dark dividing-line
to a country I have no passport to but time:
grammar not available on this frontier,
just travellers' tales and histories of navigation.
Cartographers delineate coasts and harbours
leaving the inland bare.
Will I make myself clear in your language?
are you learnable, endurable?
A foreign drink rustles on the stove.

Fireflies, star-fall of premonitions
gather in my stem: a burning spine,
silver gooseflesh in a winter labour-ward.
With an animal's determined privacy
you garden a buzzing darkness, softwalled maze
of anticipation within.
I shall become a tambourine
for winds of pain to beat.
Gravityless, spinning circular days
you prepare to wring my muscles.

I know your chemistry, that's all.
A needle sipped your world,
vertical hummingbird
to the jungle pool.
By the doctor of larch-green
your environment was named and tested,
chromatic culture interleaved in glass,
laconic significance of cells.
Weeks later
he telephoned his soundings.

The baby's all right.
It's a girl. You make me acquainted
with words and experiments
pitfalls of physiology
inhabited unknowingly till now.

My breathing is your pattern. Your own lungs
breathe inner liquid, as the Greeks supposed we do.
You make your own antiquity in here.
We have words for your wordlessness,
walled princess of the knot-garden
glinting with fat red fruit.
Dependent from amethyst and black
your spiral shining rope,
you'll approach without modesty,
a native from the vulnerable heartland
plaited deep round wayward seed
hooks of peppergrains
on white of softboiled egg.

Dusk. A light-bulb builds the bedroom round us.
Last-minute quiet.
How will you change our lives?
Daylilies glow in the half-light
on the path to the shed.
Will I be able to pause
as you're coming
if the rocks are too steep
where the green fur-flanks of the waterfall
signal a higher crescendo?
Imagination works into the night
to a last dark parapet:
that pre-historic fear
something will stay unlived.

A private journal:
why is it important?
he drew a foreign land in pencil

leaving coded notes,
relationships of colour:
rox he would write
or *blue-green . . . sandy.*
Brush-strokes of solitude:
landscape rarely rejects.

His language cheers him up.
Spindles of heat. A flickery path
between cornfields back to town.

At his lodgings
he laid in colour wash
from his private code and memory.
He liked his food,
liked children, Tennyson and jokes.
He finished off his letters home

with figures of himself
absurd, incompetent, discovering
some way of being loved

at a distance.
I have lived this landscape
that way too. A shallow valley,
secretive embroidered
mirror for a mind to sink in,
ground that steams with May.

Ian Parks

THE SWADDLED CHILD

Yorkshire, 1642

Born to parents who do not dare
to learn to love you overmuch
or breathe on you for fear
their breath disturb the flutter

of your heart, you have no life
to call your own; a thing apart
and not apart. And so the midwife,
who has known you by the score,

takes you up – your milky lips,
your bruised and wrinkled face –
enfolding you in swaddling bands.
Candles are lit; wet sheets

stripped back to the lean limbs
of your mother. Man and wife embrace.
Above your head the moon
drifts free of clouds,

and at the crossroads where the felons
hang an owlet shrieks, its talons
swooping to the kill.
Like a caught bird

in the old priest's hands
you make no sound. He dabs
his fingers in the font,
anoints your head, breathes a name.

You will know four seasons:
one bare year of blossom,
leaf-fall, snow. During which time
your father takes the cause

of Parliament in her just wars
and joins his countrymen on purple moors
whose names you will not live to learn:
your mother dies in giving birth

to brothers for your house
and is put down into the quiet earth.
But Mother Church will hold you fast
till grave-cloths swaddle you at last.

M.R. Peacocke

___

and some there be which have no memorial
such as Miss Lattimer whose son was no good
and whose hope was in the bingo caller.

Heavy Miss Lattimer with the white hand
pigmented in patches, whose large pale eyes
moistened while reading DOG THROWN FROM HIGH
    WINDOW,

Sally of the swollen knees, jumble sailor
intrepid among charity's flotsam,
what kind of memorial would you have wished?

Your joy was a little bottle of Chypre,
a plastic rose, a tabby cat that has gone
to another place, they say a better:

like you, Sally, whom I forget for months
at a time; till arbitrary things – a mop,
a sweet chemist's-counter stink – present you
solid as a monument; and then I know
that your name liveth until it's my turn.

Pascale Petit

THE SEA AT DAWN

A hopeless dawn
And the sea is high
Mother – you couldn't
Comfort me – the tide
Was always out. I cried
For days and nights
But not enough, the sea
Alone would hold
The salt in me.

You lay there
Beyond grasp
I who was born too soon,
You in your pack of ice
Rot in your womb.

I needed your love
Then, as I do now
But you had glass arms
And your tears were frost
On my case-glass.

Your drawn face is etched
On the living-room pane
And I am not born yet.
The sea is high
Your tears float there
And mix with mine

But you are locked
In a translucent zone

And it is long ago
Since we were one.
They must have implanted
Me in you, I suppose,
For no man
Could have clasped
You in their arms
Woman of snow.

I look through the window
And I am no one
Just sperm and foam.
You always wanted
Me to go
Back through the glass
Into your vulva
Your alien soul
And fling me, fling me
Back to the dark

But you can't mother
You were not able
The tide was always too cold, too far,
Forget all your tears
I don't need you mother –
– My darker face
In the old mirror,
I have another one
Whom I call day
You disappear with her.

Christopher Pilling

BICYCLE NIGHTS

Two batteries for the bicycle nights
Where your existence is by dint of red lights

To the rear; and another two illuminating
Too little to show that you're instating

Yourself in moto perpetuo on pedalling feet,
Black means of momentum down the street.

Such unseens driven by the rider's go go
Getting slower & slower & slower than slow.

The black street envelops all passenger
Traffic, each mobile being a messenger

With no message for both hands are clasped on
Handlebars that you're guiding from where you've gone

To what you're coming to — you, well on between
The immense (wind in the face) and has been.

WHAT GRETA CAN DO

(after Matisse: Portrait de Greta Prozor, 1916)

You can sit there all day in your dark blue pose,
You can keep your legs crossed,
You can envy Carmen the chance of a rose
In her hair – she was lost,
Remember, for pursuing passion to its red
Dénouement . . . You expect
Her to be consumed with ardour. Lust for bed
And flamenco infect
Your mind too. Uncrossing your legs, you can take
A leaf from her libretto,
Hitch up your midnight blue dress, tilt to a rak-
ish angle your sombrero
And, without rising from your chair, throw off your car-
can and clack your heels to a Spanish guitar.

Peter Redgrove

AT THE COSH-SHOP

Hard rubber in its silk sheath like a nightie:
The assistant offered me a small equalizer,

A Soho Lawyer that could be holstered
In a specially-tailored back pocket,

And he would introduce me to his friend
The trouser-maker. I did not think this

Necessary, but I asked, Why the silk?
It seemed luxurious for such a hard argument.

Oh, Sir, so that it will draw no blood!
He seemed surprised I asked; I thought this not right;

I believe it was the blackness
The makers did not like to show,

Like an executioner it should draw on
Lily gloves, or like a catering waiter

For an instrument that performs a religious service,
Letting the ghost out temporarily with a shriek:

While all is peace within
They steal your worldly goods

Settling the argument by appeal
To deep non-consciousness

With a swift side-swipe, the Bejasus out of him –
Or an act of sexuality, equivalent?

Do the same people make the instrument
That will stroke the Bejasus back into a person?

The silk then would be the finest, for silk chafing
Hard rubber rouses electricity, it would be

Moulded to the individual sculpt of her lover,
Providing wisely for a longish trip, could seem

Dressed in his silk pyjamas, hard and tingling,
Or as the white silky cloud conceals the thunder

And the black current
That is going to shoot its white darts up and through.

Peter Rosenberg

COVENT GARDEN

I want to live in Covent Garden
Among the rich and fancy punters
Copywriters, copytypists
Taking lunch when they appear
The fat girls in their leotards
The fat men drinking beer

I want to walk through Covent Garden
Eyes alert for all inaction
Watching from secure locations
The listless multicoloured punks
(Their frequent, great expectorations)
Buskers, painters, tramps and drunks

I want to sit in Covent Garden's
Fake *Piazza*, watching stupid
Tourists with their ugly children
Sucking on their poisoned toffee
Apples, eating fancy junk food
Drinking cups of luke-warm coffee

I want to dine in Covent Garden
Eating rich Italian food
Near pompous oafs who represent
The soiled heart of advertising's
Leather-seated chromium-plated
Offices, so patronizing

I want to shop in Covent Garden
Buying goods that no one needs
From prissy Neal Street's boutiques

Their over-price-tags not displayed
To reinforce the fantasy
Of Covent Garden's masquerade

Carol Rumens

LENINGRAD ROMANCE

1. *A Window Cut by Jealousy*
Not far from the estuary's grey window
they lit cigarettes and talked. Water kept meeting stone,
lips kept sticking to paper, time kept burning,
the lilacs were burning down to the colour of stone.
She said, I was born here, I've lived here always.
Stone kept moving in water, time kept burning,
smoke became palaces, palaces faded and faded.
My home's in Moscow, he said, my wife and children . . .
Perhaps they are just the white ash-fall of night,
perhaps they are stone. Stone kept looking at shadows,
shadows died in the white ash-fall of night.
Water kept playing with windows, time kept burning,
fingers played with the burning dust of the lilacs,
the palaces faded and faded. I've lived here always,
she said, I've friends in Moscow. Thoughts became palaces,
time went out, hands became estuaries,
the estuary was the colour of dying lilac.
They talked and lit cigarettes. Shadows flowed over the
                                                                table.
They fingered them but they didn't notice mine,
not far from the estuary's grey window.

2. *Safe Period*
He will unlock the four-hooked gate of her bra,
not noticing a kremlin built of lint,
with darkening scorch-marks where her arms press kisses.
She will pull back her arms, disturbing drifts
of shallow, babyish hair, and let him drink,
breathless, the heavy spirit smell, retreating
at length with a shy glance to grasp the chair-back,

106

and, slightly stooped, tug out the darker bandage.
Her cupped hand will glow as she carries it
quickly to the sink like something burning.
He sees the bright beard on each inner thigh,
carnations curling, ribboning in the bowl.
Her hands make soapy love. The laundered rag
weeps swift pink tears from the washing-string.
He's stiffened with a shocked assent. She breathes
against him, damp as a glass. A glass of red vodka.

Carole Satyamurti

MOUTHFULS

They lasted longer then.
Mars Bar paper crackled
as we re-wrapped half for later,
sliced the rest
to thin cross-sections,
arranged them like a wedding-cake
– loaves and fishes.

Sherbet lemons, hard against the palate,
vicious yellow. Strong sucking
made them spurt, fizz, foam,
sugar splinters lacerate
the inside of my cheeks,
surprising as ice crystals in the wind
that cut my legs through socks.

Licorice comfits, shaken in a tin,
made marching music.
Or they were fairy food
– each colour wrought a different magic:
mauve for shrinking,
green, the power to fly,
red, the brightest, eternal sleep.

The oddity of gob-stoppers:
tonguing each detail
of the surface – porcelain,
tiny roughnesses,
licking, rolling it, recapturing
the grain and silk of nipple;
rainbows glimpsed only in mirrors.

A shorter life for jelly babies
– drafted into armies, black ones last,
or wrapped in paper shawls in matchbox beds,
taken out, chewed from the feet up,
decapitated out of kindness
or, squeamishly sucked,
reduced to embryos.

William Scammell

LOOKING FOR MEL

Once off the freeway, nose-diving
round hairpins to cross the booming river
we took ourselves up into the Sierras,
lost in the high spaces of a noun.

Not quite trackless, nevertheless
dark with redwoods standing
from one Israel to the next.
Iowa Hill was the last outpost,

a wooden store whose grizzled prop
sat on his six-thousand-foot stool
thinking. His tin specs wished
you well, if you deserved it,

a moot point sweetly made. Yes
we were right for Mel, and crawled
slowly on up into the forest
that was his only known address.

The road gave out, and then the track.
There was a log across a path.
Evidently the PRIVATE PROPERTY –
KEEP OUT signs were aimed at us

and stray prospectors of the IRS
for this was gold country, staked out
and haunted since by men
whose only pension was an aching back.

A dog barked. There was Mel
shambling out of the trees, sculptor,
miner, mute and burly as a mole.

In forty years he'd sunk nine shafts

through solid rock, and found enough
to good as lacquer his wife's nails
if she'd still been around.
He poured the dust out

from a paper twist. It winked
a little, in his rocky palm,
then each grain faded back to sleep.
The guest-house was a dacha,

hand-built, one of several
dotted on his hundred-thirty acres.
A rocking chair sat
like a weathered buddha by the door.

Our bedroom smelled of pine,
must, paraffin, all happy things
to be knocked down to
at the end of a long day.

Pancakes for breakfast, a rich
breath of trees. He tossed a stone
into his flooded mine, and smiled,
and winched his shoulders straight again.

There were earthworks all around –
gardens, mineshafts, sculptured chambers
aimed at the summer solstice, where
once a year the sun might strike . . .

plans requiring another lifetime
to add to his sixty-something,
crammed with the stuff of legend
from his fighter-pilot-boyhood on.

What he scented wasn't money:
he dug the way his water-wheel
panned luscious cold new water
down by the forty-niners'

long-since-vanished flume.

FIRST SAILING

Imagine a thousand giant horseshoes
riveted together for good luck.

Imagine the decks stacked up like an in-tray,
the infant-class-drawing funnels

followed to the inch, the ton, sloping
back their ears and ready for the off.

Something is shaking the thing awake
under your feet and you race up on deck

where the wind off the Solent
flattens one side of you like a plank.

The handrail warps and judders; at a blast
of the last trump the whole ship

thinks itself into a greyhound tremble
and dreams away from the quay,

scouring a giant glass for seagulls
to scream in. The horizon turns slowly

round and proceeds to forget you
like relatives going home after a visit.

You have landed in luxury's hard lap.
Your wake stretches from here to nowhere.

Vernon Scannell

APPLE POEM

Take the apple from the bowl or bough
Or kitchen table where in gloom it glows
And you will sense, mysteriously, how
Its fragrant and substantial presence throws
A shadow shape of this one's red and green,
Whatever it may be – Rose of Bern,
Spice Pippin, Golden Russet, Hawthorn Dean –
Across the mind and then you may discern
Through every sense the quintessential fruit,
Perfected properties all apples own,
In this platonic shadow; absolute
This pleasing thing that you alone have grown.

Beneath the apple's skin, its green or gold,
Yellow, red or streaked with varied tints,
The white flesh tempts, sharp or sweet, quite cold.
Its blood is colourless; scent teases, hints
At othernesses that you can't define;
The taste of innocence, so slow to fade,
Persists like memory. This fruit is wine
And bread; is eucharistic. It has played
Its role in epics, fairy-tales, among
Most races of the earth; made prophecies
Of marriages and kept the Norse Gods young;
Shone like moons on Hesperidian trees.

And here, domestic, familiar as a pet,
Plump as your granny's cheek, prepared to be
Translated into jam or jelly, yet
It still retains a curious mystery.
Forget the holy leaves, the pagan lore

113

And that you munch on legends when you eat,
But see, as you crunch closer to the core
Those little pips, diminutive and neat
Containers aping tiny beetles or
Microscopic purses, little beads,
Each holding in its patient dark a store
Of apples, flowering orchards, countless seeds.

GRANDMA IN WINTER

In her black shawl she moves over the field of snow
With a slow proud strut, like a burgher
Or a fat crow.
The raw sun has oozed on to the lint of cloud,
A pretty smear of pain. The church gathers its little ones,
The stone children, about its skirts
And tells them an old story.

She will join them, stand perfectly still and quiet there.
No one will notice her.
And when night unfolds
Its old black umbrella with the little holes
She will pray for the blonde stones and the friable bones,
The blue melted jellies; those white
Teeth, the small blanched almonds.

HANDS

Hands can be eloquent, though sometimes they
Mislead us utterly in what they say.
I have seen slender-fingered, candle-white
Supple and fluent hands that many might
Call 'sensitive', 'a pianist's hands', 'artistic';
But these were owned by someone mean, sadistic,
Hostile to art, a gross materialist.

114

I know another man, fine pianist,
Whose powerful, sausage-fingered, meaty fists
Should hang from goal-keeper's or butcher's wrists,
Yet on the gleaming keys these hands could wake
Ghosts of drowned nightingales in starry lakes.
I knew a fighter, too, fast welterweight,
Whose punches could crack bone and could create
Sudden shattered galaxies in the head,
Yet from his hands alone you might have said
That he was not unusually strong,
For they were hairless, pale, the fingers long.
So many hands will tell us lies, but I
Have never known old labouring men's deny
Their simple character: these never lie.
For years they have manhandled spade or hook,
Shovel, axe or pick until they look
Like weathered tools, mattock, hammer, vice,
Battered, annealed by wind and sun and ice.
I like to watch them rest on tables, knees,
Lifting a pint of beer or with deft ease
Rolling a fag which later burns between
Dark oaken knuckles which have never been
Surely as soft and sensitive to pain
As this pen-pusher's hand I look at now;
But most of all I like to witness how
They lift small, tired grandchildren and hold
Them curled and safe, how gently they enfold
Their always welcome, always cherished guests,
Become protecting, gnarled and living nests.

Wendy Searle

AS SEEN ON TV

When Chris was in a head-on collision on a train
and was dragged over the dead and injured unhurt
to stand by the wreckage as rescue work took place,
her gran was shocked, her parents on Cyprus concerned.

But when her friends at school asked her: How did you feel?
What was it like? she said: It was nothing really;
I felt as though I was watching it all on TV.

Paul Sellman

WEST AFRICAN EPITHALAMION

Power coursed through her – she was juddering
   like a cranked-up generator, opposite you
   in the convulsive lights of a Lagos disco,
   nostrils flared, eyes as large as headlamps,
   your confusion satirized in the dry patois
   of her attendant friends. Her mouth opened
   in a smile of lion-yawn simplicity, revealing
   her avid tongue, her white teeth candescent with

Power coursed through her – satellite to satellite,
   pity for the starving children had surged
   through linked nations, while she had grown up
   broad and tall and fine, watching Dallas
   and dressed in designer clothes, her Daddy rich
   from Benin oil; yet calls you to her
   with a fierce shout of your name, lest you
   abandon her, her cry charged with a continent's

Power coursed through her, which also flowed
   in Mandingo girls on the slave-block, mocked for
    their
   larded braids and broad noses, priced like mares.
   She scowled at your liberal remorse, visiting
   the slavers' forts along the Atlantic, now museums;
   then, from the tower, sang sturdily out to sea
   a long dirge, as if she'd joined the huddled girls,
   their chant rising above the barracoons, flaunting its

Power coursed through her, which took you
        out of Lagos, into a Mercedes shuddering
        along a dirt road, threading the yam-plots
          and the phallic granaries. In a hut's darkness,
      her great grandmother chews on the past and spits it
        out,
      like cola nuts, remembering back a hundred years
      to the first English who conquered the kingdoms,
      north to Kano, battening like leeches on the sources
        of

Power which will course through her and you
        on your marriage night: like an Elizabethan couple,
        brought to bed by the wedding party, raucous
        and bawdy, to chants and music, your future theirs.
        Eyes as large as headlamps, nostrils flared,
        her mouth open in a smile of lion-yawn simplicity,
        she comes to you again and again, your tongues avid,
        Africa and Europe, giving and receiving

   Love, sustenance, power.

Deirdre Shanahan

OPTICS

I slunk around the house for days,
unable to drive or read.
Without glasses,
slow and dependent on you,
my eyes were adjusting back
for the test at the opticians.

The mirror revealed me as James Joyce,
suspect under the light.
Glass flicked, slides rattled
as Mr Walia selected another lens
to slot on to the iron frame
slammed across my face.

In the half-dark,
through the pretend spectacles
solid as a gun on the bridge of my nose,
it was hard to tell whether red or green was stronger.
Only the H was clear.
E, Z and Y blurred into hieroglyphics, hebrew, cities.

His doctors tried everything to improve his sight;
leeches, cocaine, bandages.
Borsch at the American hospital in Paris
performed operation on operation
getting nowhere.

Sunk in an armchair
on long afternoons, the others had to read
the proofs of *Ulysses* for him.
Later when he strolled with Paul Léon,

someone said they were,
'the lame leading the blind'.

We were like that once,
leaving the small hotel in Montparnasse
for narrow streets,
to hide in and discover secrets
from cafe tables.

Unmarried and afraid
of what the concierge would think,
I followed you,
following the map collapsed on the folds,
as we kept on ending up at the Tuileries
again and again.

FAVOURITE THINGS

There were a thousand things I wanted to say
before you put on your coat and left,
going up the street, past the laundrette, the rest of the world
and the cafe with tea stained formica
where we first met.

Don't you remember the cottage in Derbyshire?
It rained for days,
we slipped on mud and puddles
to buy eggs and milk from the farm.
Squelches. Pools of light.
Hollows holding back the sky.

There were acres of Sundays in Regents Park,
where baseball players ran.
We walked and walked miles into the afternoon
and leaving our shoes outside,
went into the Mosque;
a clearing of air, bone globe
letting slip the sky.
The circle of glass was embracing palms of night.

We, the foreigners knelt
and you were spined as the curved moon.

For three summers
we slept on the beaches of Greece and Spain.
Our words at night
the lisp of waves
falling over each other
into the deep.

Now you lie on a mattress behind shutters
the other side of the coast,
the corner where the Gods meet
and Saint Vincent lies at rest
under the largest lighthouse in Europe.

I smoke and smoke a last cigarette
reading the cinema listings.
Hours slouch like 'The Year of the Quiet Sun'
and my face feels as rough as a Polish field.

If you came back,
even now
I would tell you
that you were one of my favourite things.

Penelope Shuttle

THIEF

He will steal it, whatever you possess.
Whatever you value, what bears your name,
everything you call, 'mine', he will steal.
Everything you have is frail and will be stolen from you.
Not just watch or bracelet, ring or coat,
bright objects, soft splendours, gifts, necessities,
but the joy that bends you easily and makes you feel safe,
your love of what you see each different morning
through your window, the ordinary seen as heavenly.
Your child's power, your lover's touch, will be stolen
from under your nose. He will steal everything.
He will take everything from you. You will never see him.
You will never hear him. You will never smell him.
But he will destroy you.
No surveillance is close enough, no guard clever enough,
no lock secure enough, no luck good enough;
the thief is there and gone before you have sense
of breath to cry out.
He has robbed you before, a hundred times.
You have never seen him but you know him.
You know his vermin smell without smelling him,
you know his smile of learning without seeing it,
you feel his shadow like deprival weather, grey, oppressive.
You know he watches from far away or from just round the
       corner
as you re-gather your little hoard of riches, your modest
       share
of the world, he watches as you build your shelter of life,
your hands raw from working day and night, a house
built out of bricks that must be guessed at, groped for,
loved, wept into being; and then upon those walls

you and your people raise a roof of joy and pain, and you live
in your house with all your ordinary treasures,
your pots and pans, your weaned child, your cat and caged
   bird,
your soft bestiary hours of love,
your books opening on fiery pages, your nights full
with dreams of a road leading to the red horses of Egypt,
of the forest like a perfumed pampered room wet with
   solitude.
You forget the thief. You forget his vanity,
his sips and spoonfuls of greed. But he watches you,
sly in the vaults of his wealth.
Shameless, sleepless, he watches you.
Grinning, he admires your sense of safety.
He loves all that you love.
Then, in disguise, with empty pockets, his fingers dirty
and bare, rings of white skin in place of gold bands,
he comes like a pauper on a dark patchwork morning
when summer is turning round and robs you blind.
He takes everything.
He is the thief in whose gossamer trap you have been
   floating
all these years. He comes and takes everything.
Your house is empty and means nothing, the roof falls in
and the walls of love dissolve, made of ice;
the windows no longer watch out over heaven, the bare
   wooden
floors show their scars again and ache for the forest.
He takes everything you have, this thief, but gives you one
   gift.
Each morning you open eyes jealous as hunger, you walk
serpent-necked and dwarf-legged in the thief's distorting
   mirrors,
you go nakedly through the skyless moonless gardens and
   pagodas
of envy that he gives you, the thief's gift, your seeding
   wilderness.

Iain Sinclair

SERPENT TO ZYMURGY

more diseases than textbooks

I had thought St Vitus's dance as
much of a back number as the cakewalk:
it's stomping here in full fig,
velveteen jacket worn to flesh, pocket
torn out, like a split cheekbone

try & lift from the coop
of Old Holborn, phlegm, twitchy
parrot moods: they've even
picked up on bird diseases & foul pests

the lolling sheepheaded beaten
men, the form-filling
dole scratching, ill-tempered lumpen
mess of what we are become

this post office has more patients
than a surgery, sliding
up to the taped window across
a gob-spattered stone floor

on the low wall of the flats
a girl perfectly imitates
the 'ka-aar' of the shit-eating seagull

'ka-aar, ka-aar, ka-aar'

wait long enough:
it will be the other way around

M. Alex Smith

VERMEER: MAIDSERVANT

I imagine a calm, the ordinary
uneventful life. The pouring of milk.

The servant steadies the jug.
Upstairs, burgomasters play bass viols
while their ladies sit at virginals;
wine glasses are drained,
bourgeois fashion is high and florid.
Capital is fluid.

I imagine . . . a fiction. 'Calm was the day'
is all that we can reasonably say.

This pouring of milk
after Westphalia
after thirty years of war
after only wolves were left
to devour each other
in depopulated towns . . .

a moment of European calm.

The crust-textured loaves
irritate my palm;
I want to be a seller of bread,
to pour milk from the rough cast earthenware jug
and attain the calm
the paint has mirrored here from our unrest.

Anne Stevenson

DREAM

(After Writing on Sylvia Plath)

A glass jar rattles its split peas and pasta.
Those cysts look innocuous, but they weave
through the kernels, hatching into horrible insects.
Something's on the floor there,
buzzing like a swat wasp.
A belly like a moist rubber thimble
sucks and stings my finger. Ach, ach,
my heel reduces it to sewage.

String the creatures up, then.
Hang them on the Christmas tree.

They glisten there like fish, or softly
lengthen into milliners' feathers.
See, they are only moths, paper moths or horses,
not even paper but the Paisley curtain
sifting ashy patterns from the winter light.
Order, they order, *order*.

The flame gropes for a fire.
The dream asks meaning to patch its rags.
The flying words want paper to nest in.
Six colours arrange the white scream of the rainbow.
Even the smallest hours crawl by with a number.

These letters are marching straight into an alphabet:
X Y Z, not to infinity.

'Hotpoint welcomes you to Peterborough.'
Nobody believes it; it's only an advertisement.

'Reality welcomes you to the New World.'
Nobody believes it; it's only a poem.

LOVING RED

Blood is a colour to violate
his city cell in Hampstead.
Plush as Russia, her gifts,
woven negroid and red,
iron in the strata of the coverlet
rucked on the bed.
In heats of meeting,
an incidental crimsoning of pillowslips,
white sheets wined red.

To be naked in body
is to acquiesce willingly in red,
forced willingly to sacrifice a twilife
unacquainted with red . . .

Or so he meditates,
or might, or could,
marvelling once again
at the gender of colour,
at the rich, alien pigment,
red. Red.

Catherine Strickland

SWEETS

They were larger when I was a child,
brighter: soft-centred bonbons in garish
colours weighed by the quarter from tall
glass jars. Teacher kept them for special
occasions like the passing of exams.

I used to suck the sugar-coated ones until
the colour disappeared, the chocolate
seeped slowly through my tongue. The fizz
of sherbet lemons made me laugh. My first
lipstick was a strawberry glacier fruit.

My mother had a hidden stock of toffee twirls
for when I grazed my knee or failed to make
the hockey team. She gave me one when
I crunched a handful of pink bathsalts
mistaking them for sweets.

Now beneath the sugar-coating they're bitter
to the taste. The names are unpronounceable.
Two-tone capsules brown and red I eat at night
for sleep. Blue ones twice a day to calm me down.
Yellows 'one when required' to take the pain away.

These days I pass shop windows at a pace,
for looking in I'd see the child asking for
a gob stopper, a half of pear drops,
or watch her coming out of school
met by mother with a bag of chocolate beans.

THE PARTING

I remember how close it was
the day you left
how, down in the valley the cows stood
with fly-whisk tails swishing their flanks
and the mare gently pawing the ground.

I tried to follow you up the high road
gathering distance across the fields,
your figure getting smaller and smaller
like an eye turning to the light;
all I could see – a fence, a gate,
the river winding into nowhere,
my head turning back towards the farm.

Today it's hard to imagine any different
than the cold cavities of winter,
abandoned cottages slowly crumbling;
holes where windows had been
stare out at me across the moor –
faces in the half-light
behind a bleared white veil.

The sheep are pressed together
beneath a tracery of branches
like the blue veins that rise out of my wrists.
Hedges ragged from the wind's undoing
tilt northwards as though
the backbone of England had been broken.

A shaft of sunlight captures the last
glints of sparkle in the granite rocks
and in the frozen florets of snow.
If you'd looked back
as long as I that day
you would have seen twilight fall
and on the horizon
the sun melting into snow.

Matthew Sweeney

OMELETTES

A mattress stands on its side
with a cat asleep on top.
Behind it, the musty curtains
admit a chunk of sunlight,
while before it, a man of 70
lies, in his clothes, in a bed
and waits for the ambulance.
A tin with roll-up butts,
two cups, and a pils can
are on the floor; the smell
is of urine and damp wallpaper.
He complains of the pain
in his bandaged arm and knee,
and talks to the other bed
whose owner now is dead,
two weeks back, and looks
at me. He speaks of the hospital,
how he knows the area well –
how he lived and worked there,
a second chef in a defunct hotel,
eight years, and he asks me
how many omelettes there are,
then answers, hundreds,
and tells me the best he saw
was when he took treacle
in place of oil, and the first chef
got the omelette off intact
and he doesn't know how he did.

Raymond Tong

TRIOLET FOR ST JOHN'S

They have taken away great-grandfather's bones
    to make an office parking space.
    Having removed the old tombstones
they have taken away great-grandfather's bones.
    With desks, computers and telephones
    St John's will become a thriving place.
They have taken away great-grandfather's bones
    to make an office parking space.

Shirley Toulson

THE MONK'S TALE

Although the living here's so plain
After the softness of rich Coldingham;
I must confess, being home again
Among the sand dunes of flat Lindisfarne

Pleases me more than those soft women's ways
With food and clothing Cuthbert won't allow,
And comforts we have never dreamed of here.
It was the talk disturbed me, as you know.

So when C left his bed that second night,
I followed, hoping for a chance to speak
Of Wilfrid's Roman and disturbing schemes;
I blushed to think he may have gone to seek

Some sister out. Shamed at that thought
I tracked him down the cliff path to the shore,
Watched from behind a rock, as he strode out
Thigh-deep. Above the cold waves' roar

I heard his quiet voice grow into a shout.
He hurled the holy psalter at the sea.
Amazed, I crouched for warmth and prayed
That my base thought might be forgiven me.

All through the night his voice went thundering on,
Until the sun broke surface in the sky.
Slowly and stiffly then he came to land,
His flesh a-shiver with the cruel cold. So I

Was just about to wrap my habit round him
And warm him dry, when like a cat
That rubs your legs for food, two otters came
To give such comfort with their kindly fur that

He was soon recovered and went back
To join the nuns at matins. I went too.
He made no sign of knowing I was there.
I never spoke till now, when I tell you

This tale, and ask if you too saw,
As sands at low tide granted us their luck,
Before he greeted brothers or the abbot,
He blessed his chicken – Cuddy's eider duck.

Sylvia Turner

WHIMBERRY HILL

Elbow-deep in whimberry shrubs we crouched,
heels notched into steep turf, greaseproof-papered
picnics hidden from ruminating sheep.
For each berry posted in our picking-tins
we gorged dozens. Blue-mouthed, we clambered on
in search of fruitier patches, heads crowned
with green bracken to repel sizzling flies.
Back home, methodical mothers scalded
jars, lugged jamming-kettles up from cellars.
Strewn across the hill, indigo-fingered pickers
plucked and gathered. Grasshoppers rasped hind-legs
together, twanging aural highwires.
Purple beetles, round as ripened berries,
dumbly grasped twisted stalks. Voices
tilted on the wind, mimicking sheep-bleats
and curlew-calls. Nine-years-old, a lazy picker,
I wilted among heather clumps to watch
buzzards pair-skating over crags. Nearby,
Mrs Morgan, whimberry wizard, sat
surrounded by full baskets, eyes grounded,
busily combing a knotted bush bald
till her bent pot brimmed with berries, leaves,
beetles . . . Hefting it, she tumbled the lot
into a basket, blowing out foliage
with gale-force puffs. Gaping at her huge haul
I swallowed a grasshopper! Though I hawked
to the depths, that creature never surfaced,
a dinosaur fossil, lodged gullet-deep.
Woad-stained, we biked home, cluttered with tins.
My yield barely filled a tart, yet contained
a mouthful of inky sweetness
bleaker seasons have never depleted.

KNIGHTSBRIDGE SHOWMAN

Dulled by city traffic, I succumb
to the thrum of the underground and adopt
upright stance in the human chain feeding
the down escalators. A glimpse of *Waygood-Otis*
still intrigues: decades back, this plaque
marked for me thresholds to switchback
wizardry. Selecting my grid, I slump
one palm on the bumbling balustrade, trusting
the steel-teeth steps stay meshed at corners
as treads fold in sequence. Baggage straddled,
I slide forward, a drowsy disconnected link,
ready to plunge deep into the dungeon.

Caught napping, ears pick up a distant pitch
like pennies plopping in wishing wells.
Down there, someone is plucking a ukulele!
Now I catch the precise click of crackerjack
heels. Far below, spotlit I swear, a slick
tap-dancer occupies the deck, top-hat
flecked with pearly-king buttons and hectic
tails flapping like syncopating batons.
What zest! Flicking fingers suggest electric
dazzle. We beam as he draws us to him
by the cool clipped beat of tin-tipped toes,
the stylish tilt of happy-go-lucky feet.

The strummed ukulele throbs to orchestral
might as abruptly we're zooming down
from the stars, a string of Ziegfeld Follies
handpicked to embellish his acrobatic
tactics. A Broadway spectacular . . .
Too soon I level off, hit flat ground.
Badgered along by brisk city mobs
I lodge at last on the homeward platform
regretting Mr Otis could not be here
to see his stairway host this commanding
performance; glide-on extras recruited
for a one-off spell of instant show-biz.

135

SUPPLY TEACHER

Could *Spring* have prompted those stiff-petalled
daisies chalked on the board, abandoned
when Miss Black keeled over? Dated shoe-boxes
yield template-drawn eggs, skipping rabbits,
assembled for pasting by six-year-olds
who, uncurbed, would splash yellow houses
with box-kite windows and solid green smoke,
heedless of Nature or Mother's Day.
I'm warned that John, word-shy dreamboat, idles
anchored to pictures for hours while Vanessa
must stick with her three-times until play.
Young minds are bound to stray during broadcast
verse, so let them doodle while sums are marked.
Please yourself when you fit in proper Art,
but the caretaker draws the line at paint.
Miss Black swore by mosaics and felt pens.
Undaunted, I take charge, having shadowed
the likes of Miss Black before. Easy
to brighten so grey a backcloth, entice
supple minds out of graph-paper cages,
spotlight the stage with Magic and Life.
Vanessa finds a hedgehog. Where better
to begin? Dainty feet are marvelled at,
timid palms uncurl to test prickles.
While others dither for stencils, or beg
outlines to trace, John, unaided, tackles
a wry snout, pencils inquisitive brows,
plants a forest of spines round deep-rooted eyes.
Ten schools later I recognize that style
through smoke-tinted glass; primary colours
on skulls to out-thistle porcupine quills;
firebrands, purple haloes, cockatoo quiffs
emerge from Hair Flair Salon, as a smile
broadens to share pride in high class skills.

Val Warner

OVER THE CUPS

The sunlight dazzles me, like looking
through hair blown over the eyes, like Goldie-
locks: everything's fissured in the hair

fine cracks. An eagle, the moment hangs
'twixt cup and lip. I murmur into tepid tea, not seeing
the drowning . . . minute fly, 'If
every day were like this,' like the day,

the hour, the wild rose flowering . . . each calyx
firm, before lapsing. 'But it is
love.' And again, the cup runneth over. 'As for the weather,
this summer's near drought,' yet who wants

a wind of change, in London? He touches my hand, goes
to shepherd the kids to the bus. Errands done,
he'll take them to St James's Park, to see
Jemima Puddleduck at home on the royal lake,
the populace gathering where the wild things are,
faces merging in lapping water, whence we emerged.

BLOODY TEARS

Still down with flu, she couldn't rush
at even her snail's pace through the morning
ritual of getting herself and her school
things together. She forgot her last lesson, always

to hold a fistful of tissues like a white cabbage rose
to her nose, with her head for once proudly
tossed back. Great tears of blood spattered her patchwork
quilt from the rose of the watering-can of her nose,
so that granny-like labour by an old hand was wept over.
    Shades of
red purpled and cream pinkened, freshened

bloody rubies through the broken glass
of her tears. Thirteen-year-old veteran of so many

foster homes, 'Nothing ever makes me cry
now' was one of the first remarks volunteered to us:
for that she felt she'd burn at the bloody stake, as I
for my belief half sickness is in the mind, knowing
in my bones blood's never thicker than water.

Jane Wilson

ARTIST CONVALESCING

Sylvie with her poor lopped ribs
And her staunch lung must turn back
From our stroll, at the first slope of the mountain;
But she returns serene, among deep breaths
Of sea-dark trees where black
Damsons are putting on flesh again.

The wind is beyond measure generous,
Sweeping the last cumulus to the end
Of the washed blue. The sycamore swells,
Absorbing air into its quivering capillaries,
And blessing, as the placid leaves descend,
Sylvie's own blissful cells;

Healing, she's drawn to her easel at last.
In the clearing the pines are stacked for her autumn
Fires. Stirred by the tang of resin,
She makes for her mansion, where the sun has cast
All afternoon at one wall,
Lighting it white as a canvas. She goes in.

Kit Wright

BLOODY DRAMA

(on the play *Bloody Poetry* by Howard Brenton)

I have to tell you plainly, Mr Brenton,
That though I liked the premise of your play
And took, I think, its points, the way it went on
Entombed me in a lonelier dismay
Than if I'd spent the evening out at Prenton
Park and watched Crewe Alex draw, away,
With Tranmere Rovers, nil-nil, in the rain.
I'm glad I went. I shall not go again.

The premise? Plays do not have premises,
I know, except a stage, or overweight
With programme, they'd be their own Nemeses
And kill themselves. No plan but to *create*
For splintered truth a pointed diadem, as is
The case with these sad laurels you fixate
Upon the mind of poetry. OK,
I see I am already miles away

From any point I was about to make
But that's a hazard of *ottava rima*,
A form I follow, flailing in the wake
Of him you cast as drunkard to your dreamer,
Byron to Shelley; thus you have them take
The boards. No premise then. And yet as schemer
Of this production I emerged so glum from,
You're canny in the angle that you come from.

It is the minor figures in the *coterie*

140

That draw your bitter interest. So far,
So excellent. That Bysshe, the Super Votary
Of airy revolution, lived to scar
His acolytes on earth, you, zealous notary,
Notate with nous for where the hurt things are:
The unreality that got him plastered
Meant dreamy Bysshe was something of a bastard

In personal terms. And are there any others?
Is there authentic love that grows beyond
Immediates? To quite whom were they brothers,
These frenzied aristos? *One's* strongest bond,
It might seem, was with self: cold self that smothers
Love and dumps a dead wife in a pond.
Like any John and Jane or Dai and Blodwen,
The loves of Bysshe, though, and of Mary Godwin

Or his for Harriet, hers for him, remain
Opaque for ever and survive as mystery,
Lonesome secrets washed out by the rain
Filling the sea of European history
That will not, either, wash to shore again
The truth of Byron's fling with his half-sister. He
Leaves prurient posterity to muster
Half-lies about half-love. As does Augusta.

Such famous ghosts cannot be insulated,
However, from surmise, I quite agree.
But something in your treatment of them grated:
Too sure, too crude, too shrill, it seemed to me.
I felt their spirits had been violated.
My second, more specific beef, Beef B –
Lest that objection seem too vague and dopey:
Some of the dialogue was rather ropey.

The text, though you were properly reliant
On quoted verse and prose, was not believable
At many points, and each poetic giant
Had things to say I thought were inconceivable.
Too many clichés. Still, if I say, 'Why aren't
Their lines the goods?' it's damned hard, if achievable,
To verbalize a man who, when not dreaming,
May well have spent so much spare time in screaming.

His writing, though. Harsh years it took to do it
And this is why your play has made me sad –
The reason also why there's so much to it,
Such point and anguish: Shelley's songflame had
As aim to burn the dark world and renew it
Whole. It didn't. Doesn't. That's as mad
And blind as when he started. The malaise
Is poems don't change systems. Nor do plays.

Mark Wyatt

AFRICA

I won't be your slave any more. You
Can pull out my rocket-pad teeth, cut
Out this crocodile tongue but I'll defy
You forever. I invented mankind, you long
To forget, and intend to protect my people
Thirsty yet grateful to rhythm-plagiarizing
Musicians, for royalties from a land of milk
And honey helping me speak, I demand of your
Governments recompense for war crimes. I put
Up with Tarzan but those religious crackpots
You sent were forbidden fruit luring
Our tribes with trinkets into evil
Ways. The triangular noose placed
At Atlantic's edge still burns
In my heart, with the taunts
Of 'Gorilla' as men strived
To survive. I would rescue
Dead lions of safari snap
Fame, twist construction
Cranes in the South into
Giraffes, do as much as
I could, rebuilding a
Dream, but crippled
Badly I bemoan a
Leukaemic foot

Biographical Details

DANNIE ABSE's most recent book of poems, *Ask the Bloody Horse*, was a 1986 Poetry Book Society choice and was also selected by the Welsh Arts Council for a Literature Prize. His autobiography, *A Poet in the Family*, is available from Robson Books who have also published a critical book on his work, *The Poetry of Dannie Abse*, with contributions from Alan Brownjohn, D.J. Enright, Barbara Hardy, Peter Porter, Vernon Scannell etc.

ANNA ADAMS After thirty years in rural North Yorkshire, Anna Adams has recently returned to London, where she tends to write prose. Her most recent publications are *Dear Vincent* from Littlewood Press, *Trees in Sheep Country* from Peterloo Poets and *Six Legs Good* from Mandeville Press.

JOHN ADLARD, born in Birmingham, was educated at Midland schools and at Oxford. He has taught at universities in five European countries and at various institutions in London. His books include studies of John Wilmot Earl of Rochester, William Blake and Guillaume Apollinaire, as well as translations from French and Serbian and a long poem, *Sobieski in Autumn*.

BRIAN ALDISS has had poems published in *The TLS*, *The Times* and elsewhere. His collection of poems, *Farewell to a Child*, was published in 1982 (Priapus Press). He is better known as a writer of imaginative science fiction, and as an historian of that genre.

CONNIE BENSLEY lives in south-west London. She has had two collections of poetry published, *Progress Report* and *Moving In* (Peterloo); also two short radio plays and a short story in *P.E.N. New Fiction II*.

144

ANNE BLONSTEIN was born in Harpenden, Herts in 1958. She spent her early childhood there, and her adolescence in Surrey. She took a Natural Sciences degree, followed by a doctorate at Cambridge. She is now living and working in Basel, Switzerland.

ALISON BRACKENBURY was born in 1953. She has published two books of poetry, *Dreams of Power* (Carcanet, 1981) and *Breaking Ground* (1984). A new collection, *Christmas Roses*, is due from Carcanet in August 1988.

ALAN BROWNJOHN'S *Collected Poems* was published in 1983. His latest volume is *The Old Flea-Pit*, published by Century Hutchinson, who will issue a new, paperback edition of the *Collected* in 1988.

ELIZABETH BURNS was born in 1957 and lives in Edinburgh where she works as a bookseller. She is a member of the School of Poets, a poetry group based at the Scottish Poetry Library, who have recently published a small collection of her work.

RICHARD BURNS is an English poet, and founder of the Cambridge Poetry Festival. He is now living in Yugoslavia. Extracts are included here from *The Manager*, a three-part poem of book length, so far numbering 120 completed sections. Other books by Richard Burns include *Avebury*, *Learning to Talk*, *Tree*, *Black Light* and *Keys to Transformation*.

GILLIAN CLARKE was born in Cardiff and has lived all her life in Wales. Her most recent books are *Letter from a Far Country* and *Selected Poems*, both published by Carcanet. She moved to Cardigan-shire in 1984 to be Poet in Residence at St David's University College, Lampeter. She travels widely teaching poetry in schools, and is Chairman of the Academi Gymreig.

ELSA CORBLUTH has published poetry in many poetry magazines and anthologies and has broadcast some of her work. She has a collection, *St Patrick's Night*, forthcoming in the Peterloo Poets series (April 1988). She has won a number of poetry prizes, including joint first,

Cheltenham 1981. She has an MA in Creative Writing (Lancaster University). She lives in Dorset.

JOHN COTTON's recently published collections have been *The Storyville Portraits* (Headland), *Dust* (Starwheel Press) and *Oh Those Happy Feet!* (Poet and Printer). His poems for young people have been published in *The Crystal Zoo* (Oxford University Press) and his *New and Selected Poems* are to be published by Headland. A past Chairman of the National Poetry Society, he is currently its Treasurer and is working as the Poet in Residence at the Hertfordshire and Essex High School, Bishop's Stortford.

TONY CURTIS Born Carmarthen 1946. Senior Lecturer in English at the Polytechnic of Wales. Eric Gregory Award winner in 1972. Winner of the National Poetry Competition in 1984. His *Selected Poems* appeared in 1986 and was a Poetry Book Society Choice. As a critic he has produced *The Art of Seamus Heaney*, 1985; *Dannie Abse (Writers of Wales Series)*, 1985; *Wales – The Imagined Nation*, 1986 and *How to Study Poetry*, 1988. A new collection of poems is due shortly.

ADRIAN DANNATT was born in 1962 and lives in London.

VINCENT DE SOUZA has recently had his first four poems published in the London poetry magazine *Litmus* and he is hoping to have some more published in the near future. He is twenty-eight and works as a copywriter in London.

TIM DOWLEY is a freelance writer and lives in north London. Previous publications include *Taking Off*, an anthology of parodies, and *J.S. Bach: His Life and Times*.

STEPHEN DUNCAN is a poet and sculptor who lives and works in south London. His poetry has appeared in magazines and anthologies including the Arts Council anthologies *New Poetry* nos. 5, 6 and 7. He won a first prize for poetry in the '81 Wandsworth Literary Competition, first prize in the '85 Greenwich Festival Poetry Competition and a second prize in the '86 *TLS*/Cheltenham Festival Poetry Competition.

ANTHONY EDKINS was born in Cheshire in 1927. His publications include *The Poetry of Luis Cernuda*, New York University Press, 1971 (co-editor & co-translator) and *Worry Beads*, Peterloo Poets, 1976. A collection of poems, *Not What the Fingers Felt*, is due from Rivelin Grapheme in 1987/88.

RUTH FAINLIGHT's most recent publications are *Selected Poems* from Century Hutchinson and *Family* from Turret Books. She is now working on a new collection.

STUART HENSON received an Eric Gregory Award in 1979. His first collection, *The Impossible Jigsaw*, was published by Harry Chambers/ Peterloo Poets in 1985.

MICHAEL HOFMANN was born in 1957 in Freiburg, West Germany, and now lives in London. He has translated novels and plays from the German, and published two books of poems: *Nights in the Iron Hotel* (1983, Faber) and *Acrimony* (1986, Faber).

DONALD HOPE was born in Birmingham in 1932 and now lives in London. He is married with two children. He has published occasional poems in the *New Statesman*, *The Times Literary Supplement*, the *New Review* and the *Literary Review*. He is the brother of the late Francis Hope.

MICHAEL HOROVITZ's latest book is *Midsummer Morning Jog Log*, a 670-line rural rhapsody illustrated by Peter Blake, from Five Seasons Press, Madley, Hereford HR2 9NZ in three beautifully produced editions. The double issue 17–18 of his *New Departures* series should be out early '88 as *Grandchildren of Albion* – first of several anthologies of recent alternative poetries in Britain.

THOMAS CYRIL HUDSON was born in Cowes, in 1910. He has contributed articles and poems to various newspapers and magazines, and his radio play *Murder Remembered* was broadcast by the BBC in 1970. He has received various awards, including an Arts Council prize for poetry.

147

PETER HUGHES was born in Oxford in 1956. He went to schools there before studying art and literature and then doing an M. Litt in Modern Poetry in English. For the last three years he has lived in Italy where he teaches English. A pamphlet of his poetry was published by the Many Press in 1983.

NICKI JACKOWSKA has had four collections of poetry published, the most recent being *Gates to the City* (Taxus Press). She has also developed a career as a novelist, her third novel *The Islanders* being published in March 1987, to coincide with a residency at Brighton Festival. She tutors regularly for eg. Arvon Foundation, and gives frequent readings.

ALAN JENKINS was born in 1955, in London, where he currently lives. Since 1980 he has been on the staff of *The Times Literary Supplement*, and is Fiction and Poetry Editor for that paper. His poems and reviews have appeared in *The TLS*, the *Observer*, *Sunday Times*, *New Statesman* and *Encounter*, and in *New Chatto Poets* (1986). His first collection will appear from Chatto and Windus in 1988.

ANNE MARINA JONES was born in 1934 in a village south of Birmingham. In 1956 she emigrated to Canada, returning in 1960 to reside in Peterborough from where she has travelled widely. She began writing for her children and eventually for a local newspaper. Several of her poems have been accepted and published in magazines, read on Radio Cambridge and one will appear in the new *American Poetry Anthology*.

SYLVIA KANTARIS's most recent books of poetry include *The Tenth Muse* (Peterloo 1983/Menhir, 1985); *News from the Front* (in collaboration with D.M. Thomas, Arc Publications, 1985) and *The Sea at the Door* (Secker & Warburg, 1985). She has also collaborated with Philip Gross on *The Air Mines of Mistila* (Bloodaxe, 1988) and her latest solo collection is due shortly. She lives, writes and teaches in Cornwall.

ROY KELLY's first collection of poems, *Drugstore Fiction*, was published by Peterloo Poets in 1987. An essay appeared in *All Across*

148

the Telegraph: A Bob Dylan Handbook (Sidgwick & Jackson 1987). Stories and plays have also appeared on BBC Radios 3 and 4. He is less successful than he would like, and a little older than he looks.

JAMES KIRKUP's latest British publications are *The Sense of the Visit* and *Fellow Feelings* (Gay Men's Press). Other publications include *Ecce Homo: My Pasolini, No More Hiroshimas, Zen Contemplations* and *The Guitar Player of Zuiganji*. Among his many translations are *Modern Japanese Poetry* (University of Queensland Press) and the Kabuki opera *An Actor's Revenge*. He has been Professor of Comparative Literature at Kyoto University of Foreign Studies, Japan, since 1976.

STEPHEN KNIGHT was born in 1960, in Swansea, and read English at Jesus College, Oxford. Poems have appeared in *London Magazine*, the *New Statesman, The Times Literary Supplement* etc and been broadcast on Radio 3. A selection appears in *Poetry Introduction 6* (Faber, 1985). In 1987, he received a major Gregory Award.

LOTTE KRAMER was born in Mainz, Germany, and came to England as a child refugee in 1939. She did all kinds of work (laundry hand, lady's companion, shop assistant) while studying Art and History of Art in evening classes. She began to write in 1970, and has been widely published. Her most recent collections are *Family Arrivals, Ice-Break, A Lifelong House* and *The Shoemaker's Wife* (Hippopotamus Press).

MAUREEN GUYAN LALOR was born in Aberdeen and is a graduate of King's College University of Aberdeen. She is a lecturer in twentieth-century English and American fiction, living in Devon, married to a marvellous, wild Irishman. She has three grown-up children and loves foreign travel and moving home.

JOHN LATHAM is a physicist. Two volumes of his poetry were published by Harry Chambers/Peterloo Poets: *Unpacking Mr Jones* (1982) and *From the Other Side of the Street* (1985). He has had several poems broadcast on 'Poetry Now' (BBC Radio 3) and is the winner of several poetry competitions.

SARAH LAWSON was born in Indianapolis, Indiana, in 1943 and has lived in Britain since 1967, when she came as a student to Glasgow. Her poems have appeared in numerous poetry magazines and anthologies, including *Poetry Introduction 6* (Faber). She has translated Christine de Pisan's *Treasure of the City of Ladies* from medieval French for Penguin Classics. She is currently writing a series of poems about Holland.

ROBIN LEANSE was born in Nassau, Bahamas in 1951. He first published in the *Bananas Literary Magazine* in 1979. He was a major prizewinner in the Crouch End Arts Festival in 1985, and has had work in *Ambit Magazine*. He lives in London and is currently working on a long narrative poem and the libretto for an opera *The Ship of Fools*.

KEITH LINDSAY was born in Birmingham in 1956, and despite this still chose to write poetry. He lives in Staffordshire and is co-editor of a small poetry magazine, *Bull*. He is also one half of a poetry performance duo, Brummie Brothers, and an actor, scriptwriter, folksinger and driver of fast cars. He did not go to Oxbridge, does not know Craig Raine and is too old now for a Gregory.

ADAM LIVELY was born in 1961. He studied history and philosophy at Cambridge and at Yale University in America. Since then he has worked as an editor at William Heinemann and has just had a novel, *Blue Fruit*, published.

PROFESSOR ROY MACGREGOR-HASTIE (MA PhD etc) is Dean of the American Universities Graduate School in Europe; for a score of years he was the senior British *collaborateur* at UNESCO. He is the author of several books of verse translation in the UNESCO Collection of Representative Works, as well of popular biographies including those of General Gordon (1985) and Nell Gwyn (1987).

MAIRI MACINNES was born in County Durham in 1925. She was educated in Yorkshire and at Oxford. She is married with three children. She went to the USA in 1959. She has published two volumes of poetry: *Splinters* (University of Reading, 1953) and

Herring, Oatmeal, Milk & Salt ('Quarterly Review of Literature' series, 1981).

RUTH MORSE was born in Cambridge, Mass. in 1948. She has taught at the Universities of London, Sussex and Leeds, and held Fellowships at the Humanities Research Centre of the Australian National University, the Australian National Library and the Universidad Simon Bolivar in Caracas, Venezuela. Her poems have appeared in the *Cumberland Poetry Review, Shenandoah* and the *Southern Review* in the US; the *Literary Review, Outposts, PN Review* and *Verse* in England; and *Quadrant* in Australia. She is currently Leathersellers' Fellow in English at Fitzwilliam College, Cambridge, where she has lived since 1970.

CHRISTINA MUIRHEAD Born 1944 in Liverpool. Now living in Preston and working as a bursar in a high school. Attended several writing courses and had a one-act play performed at Preston's Charter Theatre in 1984. Started writing poetry in 1986.

PAUL MUNDEN was born in Poole, Dorset in 1958. He graduated from York University in 1980 and formed the Jazz & Poetry group 'Tortoise' with Oliver Comins. He was awarded a Writer's Bursary by Yorkshire Arts Association in 1982, and now runs a writers' workshop for York University. His poems have appeared, or are to appear in *Encounter, Grand Piano, Iron*, the *Literary Review*, the *London Magazine* and the *New Writer*.

RUTH PADEL was born in 1946. She has lived mainly in Oxford, London and Greece, and has taught Greek in universities while finishing a twenty-year book on mind and metaphor in tragedy (forthcoming OUP). She is married and has a small daughter. She has published poems in *The Times Literary Supplement, Encounter, PN Review, Kenyon Review* etc and in various pamphlets (*Alibi*, Many Press, 1985). She has also written many reviews and articles on literature, madness and religion, especially in connection with Greece.

IAN PARKS was born in 1959 in Mexborough, South Yorkshire. His first collection, *Gargoyles in Winter*, which received a Yorkshire Arts

Award, was published by Littlewood Press in 1985. He is married and lives in Scarborough where he has been Writing Fellow at North Riding College of Education since 1986.

M.R. PEACOCKE was born in 1930. Having brought up a family and worked variously as a teacher, social worker and counsellor, she is now trying to combine writing with running a smallholding in Cumbria. She has won several poetry prizes in the last two years and her first collection, *Marginal Land*, is due from Peterloo Poets in early 1988.

PASCALE PETIT's poems and short stories have been published by *Iron, Writing Women, Strange Maths, Graffiti, Litmus, Angels of Fire Radical Poetry Anthology* (Chatto & Windus). Her sculptures were exhibited in 'Pandora's Box' 1984–86, nationwide, and were featured on television in Marina Warner's 'Imaginary Women' programme and were in 'Fresh Art' (Nicholas Treadwell) in 1986 at the Barbican. She is presently at the Royal College of Art, and will hold her MA sculpture exhibition in the near future.

CHRISTOPHER PILLING won the New Poets Award in 1970 with *Snakes & Girls* and in 1983 the Kate Collingwood Award with his first play *Torquemada*. For years he has been translating Tristan Corbière's *Les Amours Jaunes*, and a snippet appears in the *Oxford Book of Verse in English Translation* (1980). He lives in Keswick where he teaches French.

PETER REDGROVE's most recent books of poetry are *The Moon Disposes: Poems 1954–1987* and *In the Hall of the Saurians* (both Secker and Warburg, 1987). He has also published this year *The Black Goddess and the Sixth Sense* (Bloomsbury, 1987) a poetry and science manifesto. He lives in Cornwall with Penelope Shuttle – co-author of their revolutionary study of the menstrual cycle *The Wise Wound* (Grafton 1978) – and they have a daughter, Zoe.

PETER MICHAEL ROSENBURG was born in London in 1958 and graduated from the University of Sussex in 1979. Between 1980–85 he travelled to forty countries around the world, working seasonally as a tour guide in Europe and North America. He began his first novel in 1984. His second novel, a collaboration entitled *The Usurper*, is to be published by Grafton in 1988. His third novel, *Daniel's Dream*, was recently completed. He is currently working on another novel, and on the screenplay for *The Usurper*.

CAROL RUMENS has published five collections of poetry, the latest being *Selected Poems* (Chatto & Windus, 1987). Her first novel, *Plato Park*, was also published in 1987. She is working on a new collection of poems about Leningrad.

CAROLE SATAYAMURTI has published poems in a number of magazines and anthologies. She was the winner of the 1986 National Poetry Competition. Her first collection, *Broken Moon*, is published by Oxford University Press. She teaches sociology at North-East London Polytechnic, and lives in London with her teenage daughter.

WILLIAM SCAMMELL's most recent books are *Eldorado* (Peterloo Poets, 1987) and a critical study of *Keith Douglas* (Faber, 1988). He received the Cholmondeley Award from the Society of Authors in 1980.

VERNON SCANNELL ws born in 1922. He has published many books of poems, including *New and Collected Poems, 1950–1980* (Robson Books).

WENDY SEARLE was born in South Africa of British parents and read English and History at Natal University. She has worked as a library assistant, reading instructor and now earns her living as secretary to an antiques dealer. She has three daughters and lives in London.

DEIRDRE SHANAHAN was born in London in 1955 and studied English at University College, North Wales. She has taught, and now lives and works in London. She has had poems published in numerous journals and periodicals, including *Encounter*, *Poetry Review* and the *Literary Review*. She won a Gregory Award in 1983.

PENELOPE SHUTTLE's most recent collection of poetry appeared in 1986, *The Lion from Rio*, from OUP. Her work has appeared in numerous magazines and anthologies, including *The Penguin Book of Contemporary British Poetry* and *No Holds Barred*. She also publishes novels and short stories, and is co-author of the pioneer study of menstruation, *The Wise Wound*, reissued by Grafton Books in 1986. She is married to Peter Redgrove and has a young daughter.

IAIN SINCLAIR lives in east London, from where he has published eleven books, including *The Birth Rug* (1973), *Lud Heat* (1975) and *Suicide Bridge* (1979). His first novel, *White Chappell, Scarlet Tracings* (1987) was published in hardback by Goldmark (of Uppingham): the paperback by Paladin, who will also publish his selected poems, under the title *Autistic Poses*.

M. ALEX SMITH was born in 1944 and is married with a daughter. He has always worked in the City in Stockbroking and Merchant Banking. Apart from literature, his main interests are history, economics and music. He assisted with a poetry magazine, *Poetry One*, in the heady sixties.

ANNE STEVENSON, an American poet long resident in Britain, has just published her *Selected Poems*, 1954–84 with OUP. *Bitter Fame*, her poet's biography of Sylvia Plath, will appear from Penguin and Houghton-Mifflin in 1988.

CATHERINE STRICKLAND was born in 1953 in Essex. She read English at the University of Warwick. She works in an art gallery and lives in Oxford.

MATTHEW SWEENEY was born in Donegal in 1952. He moved to London in 1973 and has lived there ever since. He has published three collections of poetry to date, the most recent of which – *The Lame Waltzer* (Allison and Busby, 1985) – was a Poetry Book Society Recommendation. He won the 1986 Writing Fellowship at the University of East Anglia.

RAYMOND TONG is a retired British Council officer. He has written and edited a number of books, his most recent collection of poems being *Crossing the Border*, published by Hodder and Stoughton in 1978. In the past few years his poems have appeared in many periodicals, including *Encounter*, *New Statesman* and the *Spectator*.

SHIRLEY TOULSON was born in 1924 and owes her education to Birkbeck College. Formerly a London-based journalist, she now keeps her cat and books in Somerset where she spends the winter months writing. During the rest of the year, she travels in order to research the topographical/historical books which she has been working on since 1974.

SYLVIA TURNER was born in mid-Wales in 1933 and was educated at Bath Academy of Art. She is a contributor to *Outposts*, the *Scotsman*, *Poetry Nottingham*, *Proof*. She is an author of children's books (as Sylvia Fair) including the picture book *The Bedspread* (Macmillan, 1982). She has five children and is currently married to the poet and novelist Bill Turner. She lives in Lincoln.

VAL WARNER is a freelance writer who translated Corbière – *The Centenary Corbière* (Carcanet) and edited *Collected Poems and Prose of Charlotte Mew* (Carcanet/Virago). She has received a Gregory Award for Poetry. Her poetry books are: *Under the Penthouse* (Carcanet) and *Before Lunch* (Carcanet, 1986). She has published short stories in *Encounter*, *P.E.N. New Fiction* II, *Serievins* etc and is currently working on a novel.

JANE WILSON was born in Hampshire and is grandmother of two Northumbrians. Contributor to many magazines and anthologies. *With Love* published by Littlewood Press in 1987. Three composers have set her verse to music. One radio play broadcast, and a stage play – *Close-Ups of a Wreck in Progress* due to be presented a Soho Poly Theatre in 1988.

KIT WRIGHT An earlier collection of Kit Wright's, *The Bear Looked down over the Mountain*, was a Poetry Book Society Recommendation, joint winner of the Geoffrey Faber Memorial Award and winner of the

Alice Hunt Bartlett Prize. Born in Kent in 1944 and educated at Oxford, he lectured at a Canadian university for three years, and has been a Fellow Commoner of Trinity College, Cambridge. He was one of the six British poets chosen to tour the USA to celebrate the Bicentennial in 1976. Kit Wright is well known as an author and editor of children's poetry. He has also published *Bump-starting the Hearse* (Hutchinson 1983). Hutchinson will publish *Poems 1974–1983* in October 1988.

MARK WYATT was born in Guildford, Surrey in 1959. He has had over forty poems published in twenty periodicals which include *Acumen, Iron, Litmus, New Statesman, Outposts, PN Review, Poetry Durham, Prospice, Rialto, The Times Literary Supplement*. He will soon be editing a new magazine.